How to Build a

FIBERGLASS CAR

PUBLISHED BY
FLOYD CLYMER
LOS ANGELES

$1.00

HOW TO BUILD A FIBERGLASS CAR

By W. I. Boyce-Smith, Manufacturer
of the Victress - at 203.105 mph,
the world's fastest sports car.

And Edmond Kelly, President, Allied
Products Engineering Corporation,
fiberglass and resin distributors.

Drawings by

Hugh Jorgensen

FLOYD CLYMER PUBLICATIONS

World's Largest Publisher of Books Relating to
Automobiles, Motorcycles, Motor Racing, and Americana

1268 SO. ALVARADO STREET, LOS ANGELES 6, CALIFORNIA

INTRODUCTION

Welcome to the world of digital publishing ~ the book you now hold in your hand, while unchanged from the original edition, was printed using the latest state of the art digital technology. The advent of print-on-demand has forever changed the publishing process, never has information been so accessible and it is our hope that this book serves your informational needs for years to come. If this is your first exposure to digital publishing, we hope that you are pleased with the results. Many more titles of interest to the classic automobile and motorcycle enthusiast, collector and restorer are available via our website at www.VelocePress.com. We hope that you find this title as interesting as we do.

NOTE FROM THE PUBLISHER

The information presented is true and complete to the best of our knowledge. All recommendations are made without any guarantees on the part of the author or the publisher, who also disclaim all liability incurred with the use of this information.

TRADEMARKS

We recognize that some words, model names and designations, for example, mentioned herein are the property of the trademark holder. We use them for identification purposes only. This is not an official publication.

INFORMATION ON THE USE OF THIS PUBLICATION

This manual is an invaluable resource for the classic 50's and 60's fiberglass "kit car" enthusiast and a "must have" for owners interested in designing and building their own fiberglass bodies. While the content focuses on one particular car from that era the information is universal in its application. However, in today's information age we are constantly subject to changes in common practice, new technology, availability of improved materials and increased awareness of chemical toxicity. As such, it is advised that the user consult with an experienced professional prior to undertaking any procedure described herein. While every care has been taken to ensure correctness of information, it is obviously not possible to guarantee complete freedom from errors or omissions or to accept liability arising from such errors or omissions. Therefore, any individual that uses the information contained within, or elects to perform or participate in do-it-yourself repairs or modifications acknowledges that there is a risk factor involved and that the publisher or its associates cannot be held responsible for personal injury or property damage resulting from the use of the information or the outcome of such procedures.

It is important that the reader recognizes that any instructions may refer to either the right-hand or left-hand sides of the vehicle or the components and that the directions are followed carefully. One final word of advice, this publication is intended to be used as a reference guide, and when in doubt the reader should consult with a qualified technician.

FOREWORD

Throughout the United States, from home garages to the great auto centers in Detroit, fiberglass cars are being built. A natural outgrowth of the steel or aluminum body, fiberglass allows a freedom of design never before available to the body builder. Probably the greatest single advantage of fiberglass is that any one with ingenuity and perserverance can build a car body according to his own ideas without expensive tools.

This booklet is offered with the idea of describing the general methods of fabricating glass car bodies to the end that the means and the materials are made known to everyone interested. By the application of this information and the combination of effort and ingenuity, fiberglass car bodies can be built by the average person without previous experience.

It must not be expected that a car body can be made without a certain amount of determination. The use of fiberglass is a matter of technique which is readily acquired but not without some actual experience of handling the materials involved. It would be impossible to expect to build a house from directions received in a book if the individual had no knowledge of the use of a hammer or saw. But the advantage of fiberglass is that where the building of a house is far more complex than the ability to use the hammer or the saw, the use of fiberglass on the other hand is relatively simple and when the minimum techniques have been acquired great progress can be made without the necessary assimilation of still further techniques. The main thing is to know the materials required and the mistakes to avoid.

Dedicated to

A Young Industry

THE VICTRESS mounted on 41 Ford chassis manufactured by Victress Manufacturing Company from fiberglass and marko resins.

THE VICTRESS
World's Fastest Sport Car

INDEX

F.	FOREWORD	PAGE NUMBER
I.	FIBERGLASS MATERIALS	1

    1. Resins
    2. Fiberglass
        a. Cloth
        b. Matte
        c. Treatment

II. CAR BODY STYLING   5

    1. Sketching
    2. Models

III. MOCK-UP (MALE MOLD)   7

    1. Blow up
    2. Station Formers
    3. Building
    4. Use of Materials
        a. Wire
        b. Plywood
        c. Plaster

IV. PRODUCTION MOLDS (FEMALE MOLD)   13

    1. Fiberglass
    2. Calcerite

V. MAKING THE BODY   21

    1. Preparing the Mold
        Parting Agents
    2. Fiberglass Structure
    3. The Body
    4. The Hood
    5. Doors

VI. ATTACHING BODY   29

    1. Sub-Structure
    2. Hardware

VII. TRIMMING   33

VIII. FINISHING   33

    1. The Scope and the Challenge
    2. Attachments
        a. Windshield
        b. Lights
        c. Accessories
    3. Upholstery
    4. Deck Board
    5. Paint

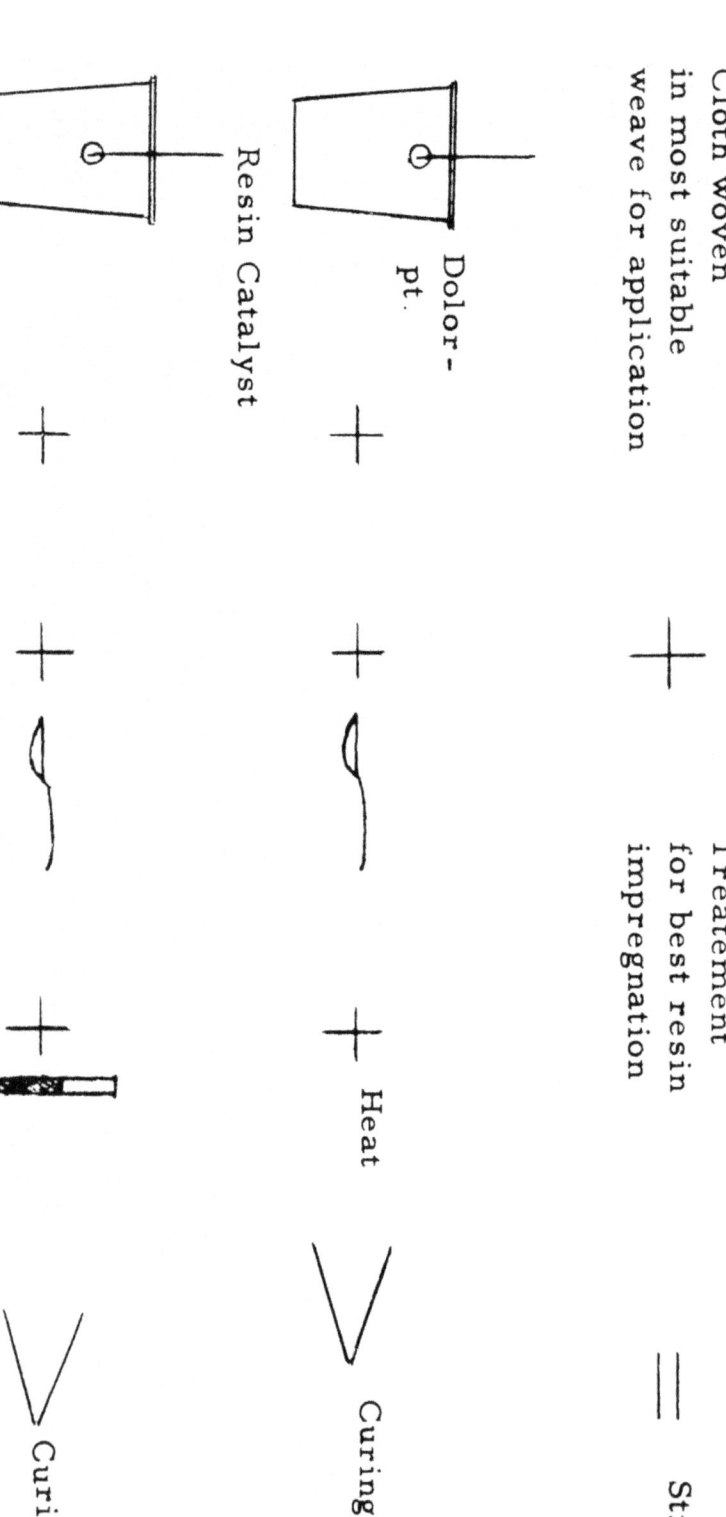
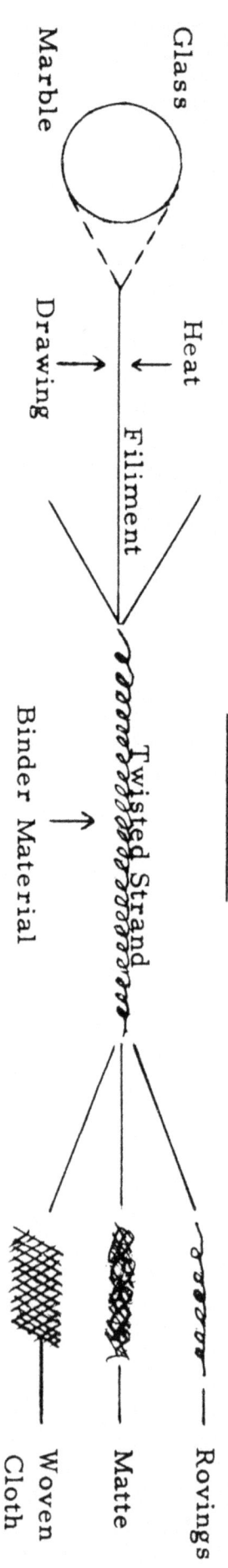

SKETCH I

FIBERGLASS MATERIALS

A little fundamental knowledge of fiberglass and resins cannot but help the individual in their use. Probably the best way of describing the process would be to refer back to the method of construction in which concrete is reinforced by steel. Concrete is a very easy product to use and yet because of its brittleness it must be properly reinforced by steel. Here a thorough knowledge of the properties of the concrete and methods of reinforcing it are essential to the engineering of a structure to be built. This is a simple illustration and yet fiberglass is essentially the same as we are going to use polyester resins in the place of concrete, and the resins, though easy to use, are relatively brittle unless they are properly reinforced. Here, however, we use glass instead of steel.

(Sketch 1)

RESINS

Synthetic resins take many forms among which are the phenolics, the ureas, the acrylics, the epoxies and the polyesters. Polyesters are selected for use in building car bodies, boats, aircraft parts and many other structural and decorative items because they cost less and are easy to use and to control.

Polyester resins are heavy liquid (9 pounds per gallon) of viscosity varying from 75 cps to 70,000 cps which, in other words, means from water to heavy molasses. A resin of approximately 700 cps has been selected and recommended for the use in car bodies mainly because it is easy to work with and, as will be shown later, "wets-out" fiberglass cloth and matte most readily.

In order to create a solid from this liquid it is only necessary to add a catalyst and then subject the catalized resin to heat ($200°F$ for about two hours). Resin, thus catalized, will retain its liquid form for several days and this is known as "pot life". Eventually the catalyst will start working on the resin even without the application of heat and the entire mass will turn from liquid to solid. This is brought about because the catalyst creates an exothermic heat which is a chemical heat created within the resin itself. This heat cures the resin and turns it from a liquid to a solid. The average individual does not have large ovens available to create heat to cure resins but he may accomplish the same by adding to the catalized resin an accelerator. The accelerator, in a relatively short time, "kicks over" the catalyst and the exothermic heat is brought about far more rapidly. By the judicial use of the catalyst and accelerator the curing time can be controlled and brought about as desired. It is also to be remembered that because exothermic heat is greater in a mass, resin will set up, or cure, in a pot before this cycle occurs with resin spread out over a part. Therefore, when accelerators are used, only a limited amount of resin can be mixed in advance. The most common formulation of resin plus catalyst plus accelerator is approximately 2% of catalyst and accelerator by weight added to the resin. If a fine quality resin is used and care is exercised as to the proper

RESINS (Cont.)

measurement of the catalyst and accelerator the same curing cycle can be expected each time. One thing, however to know, is that the room temperature in which the part is curing will have considerable effect on the cure. Any given formulation will cure more rapidly on a hot day than if the surrounding temperature is cool. Here again experience will permit the operator to vary the amount of catalyst and accelerator used so that even in the hottest weather or under coolest conditions he may predetermine his pot life and curing cycle. Going back to the 2% formulation, at 70° room temperature the pot life will be about 40 minutes and the curing cycle 2 hours. Starting with this, the individual will vary the amount of catalyst and accelerator to suit his operation and the temperature conditions in which he is working.

It is important in selecting resins to consider only those resins which will cure properly at room temperature. Some resins do not cure thoroughly on the surface, others are inhibited by air and will never cure on the surface. The surface cure is most essential as a certain amount of sanding must be done on the final surface of the car body.

FIBERGLASS

It is just as important to properly reinforce with fiberglass as it is to get a correct cure of the resin. Many fiberglass materials are available and they must be discussed with regard to the purposes of their use, the ultimate strength as a laminate and, of course, with regard to the economical side of the matter.

The basic producers of glass fibers, through their use of heat and pressure on glass in marble form, are able to produce long filaments which are then bunched one way or another in very much the same way as thread is made. These are called fibers or rovings. For ease of handling a binder is sometimes added to the individual filaments. The field of making glass and the subsequent operation of turning it into a cloth, though most interesting, is, however, a science complete in itself and has no proper place in this book except to inform and warn the glass car body builder that the use of wrong materials in reinforcing resin can be just as disastrous as the improper use of steel in reinforcing a concrete wall.

CLOTH

By and large, there are two divisions of glass material which are used in car bodies: the woven glass cloth and the glass matte. The weaving of glass cloth is almost identical to the weaving of any other material and is done on large looms by various weavers throughout the country. Innumerable varieties of strength are accomplished by the amount of glass contained in a square inch of cloth, the methods in which the threads are actually woven and the ability of the resin to impregnate the cloth. It is therefore most important that a cloth of sufficient strength be selected by the car body builder with the view that the ultimate laminate will be of adequate strength to carry the loads required and still not be excessively expensive. Fiberglass cloths recommended for car body builders are of a substantial thickness, from 11 to 15 thousands of an inch, and yet of a moderately open weave so that the resin may penetrate the cloth thoroughly. Some cloths are woven expressly for the purpose of being used in presses and with heat cures. These cloths may be stronger within themselves but are not the best to use in hand lay up especially where room temperature cures are necessary. The operator has not the ability or time to thoroughly wet-out the cloth and thereby make a strong part. It is also essential that an adequately substantial cloth is used, as having too little glass content in the laminate will result in a weak, thin or brittle finished product. The various forces effecting this operation have been closely studied by the cloth and resin manufacturers and through their experience and their recommendations there is no real problem to select the proper cloth for this use.

MATTE

The other fiberglass product which will be used by most car body manufacturers is matte. This material is designed to economically give thickness to a laminate. Although not as strong a reinforcing material, it is of adequate strength when used in proper combination with resin and fiberglass cloth and thick sections are built up at far less cost than would be incurred by means of several layers of woven cloth. By and large, matte is a mass of unoriented glass fibers and various binders are used to hold these together until they are impregnated with resin. Quite recently, there have been some new developments in making of matte which deserve consideration because they have greatly increased the strength that can be expected. This has been accomplished by the controlling of the direction of the glass fibers in a matte so that they all run one way. Thus great strengths are obtained in the one direction and by using one layer of matte going north and south and the other layer east and west, a stronger laminate can be developed than by the use of the multi-directional mattes. Carrying the thought still further, there are some interesting cloths (glass material made by the simple weaving of roving) which are a bundle of glass filaments. All of this is to achieve the desired thickness in the laminate.

The best method to obtain the proper laminate for a car body is the use of one layer of woven fiberglass cloth, the building up of thickness by the addition of one or more layers of glass matte and finally another layer of woven fiberglass cloth. This is what is meant by making a laminate or sandwich. The actual process of lay up will be described in the part of this book that deals with the actual fabrication of a car body.

TREATMENT

Most woven cloths of fiberglass are now found with one of various treatments on the surface. Not too much is known by the public concerning these treatments, how they are accomplished or their real purpose. The overall purpose of treating fiberglass cloth is to make it so that it will readily soak up resin when it is applied. The most common combination of treatments are the 112 and the 114. This is known as the 114 treatment and is a development of the Du Pont Company. First the 112 treatment is applied by passing the cloth through towers in which it is subjected to heat blasts. This process cleans the cloth and removes the oils which are necessary in the weaving. After the 112 treatment, the 114 treatment is applied resulting in a chromed surface of the cloth. Together this combination makes the cloth far more easy to impregnate and is a must for car body laminators. The cost of treated cloths is about ten percent higher than the untreated material and is certainly worth the difference.

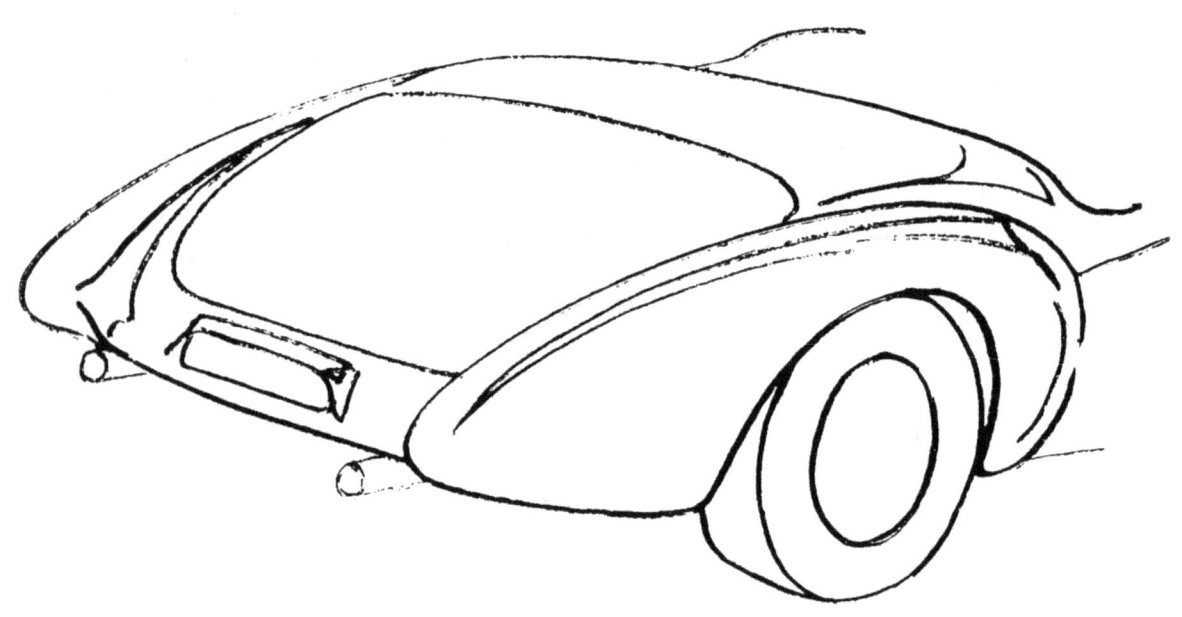

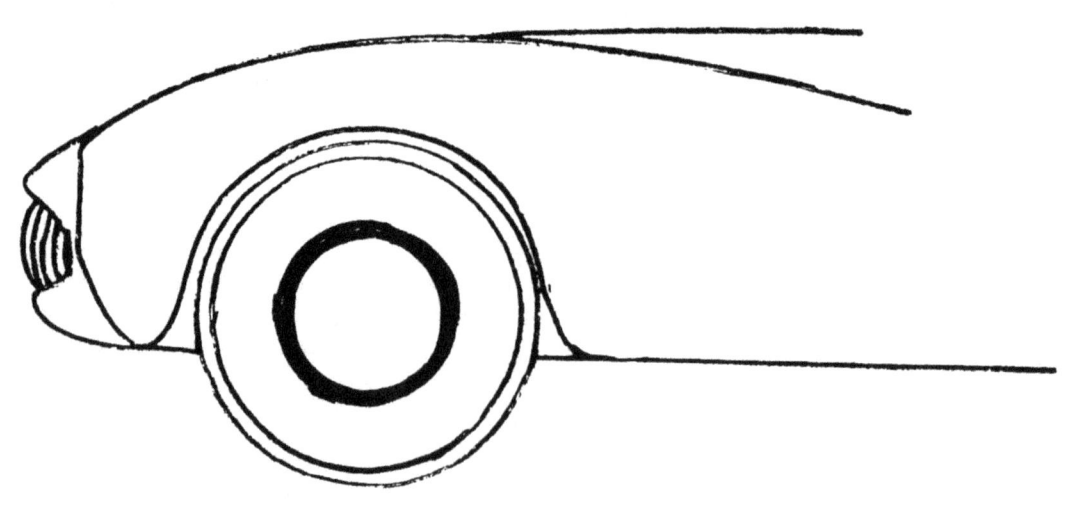

(Sketch 2)

STYLING

There are no hard and fast rules concerning automobile styling. It is largely a matter of the individual taste and preference. What appears to be a good looking style to one person may repel another. However, there are some general hints to the beginning designer which may prove useful.

It takes a certain spark of real genius to create a truly new style. It is seldom accomplished by any beginner. Therefore the best thing for the beginning automobile stylist is to take parts and bits from cars already in production and modify them to suit his own particular tastes. This may appear to be copycat type of redisigning or rehashing an existing style, however, certain lines are fundamental. The automobile has four wheels and their position is pretty well predetermined. There is very little leeway in general parts of the body design, the stylist has only the selection of certain basic curves, particularly in the nose area, the shaping of the fenders, the shaping of the tail assembly, the development of the windshield and top, etc.

If any existing popular style will be closely analyzed, it will be discovered that in many ways it is similar to cars already on the road. The individuality of any particular car comes from combining basic lines into one smooth flowing pattern. Therefore, the best approach for the budding car stylist is to use lines similar to, but not identical to, existing cars. Individuality may be easily expressed in the smaller areas such as the grill, fender lines or trunk section.

After you have a fairly good idea of what your basic style is going to be, start your sketching. The simplest way to do this is to lay out your chassis first, draw the wheels in the position in which they will be on the

(Sketch 2) See Page 4

car, draw in the frame at the height it will be from the ground, add other components such as the radiator, the motor height: position the steering gear and transmission. You can draw up half a dozen of these sketches to start with. After you have this basic layout start drawing your automobile body over the mechanical components which must be accommodated. If you can draw in three dimensions draw as many views as possible to get a more general idea of what your style is going to look like. After you are satisfied with your basic style, the next step is to make a one quarter size clay model of your proposed car. Artists' clay and tools may be procured from any artists' supply store. The simplest way to make the model is to rough form a piece of wood into the general shape slightly smaller than the automobile you propose to design. Clay may be applied to the outside of

(Sketch 3) See Page 6

the basic wooden form and used in developing your contours. Drill 1/4" holes into the surfaces of the wood for the clay to anchor into. It is important that the model be at least one quarter full size so that it may be large enough to observe contours carefully. Photographs of the completed clay model will help in this study. Place the model in realistic surroundings and photograph it, this will give a more definite idea of what the finished automobile will look like.

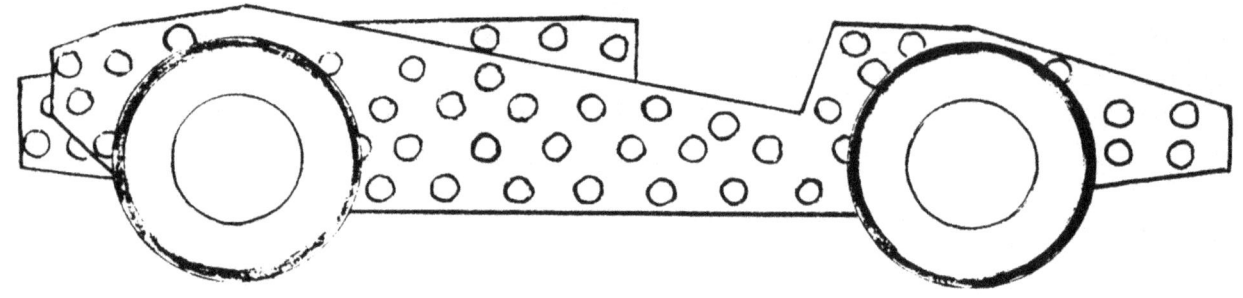

1. Wood buck with 1/4" holes drilled for anchor of clay.

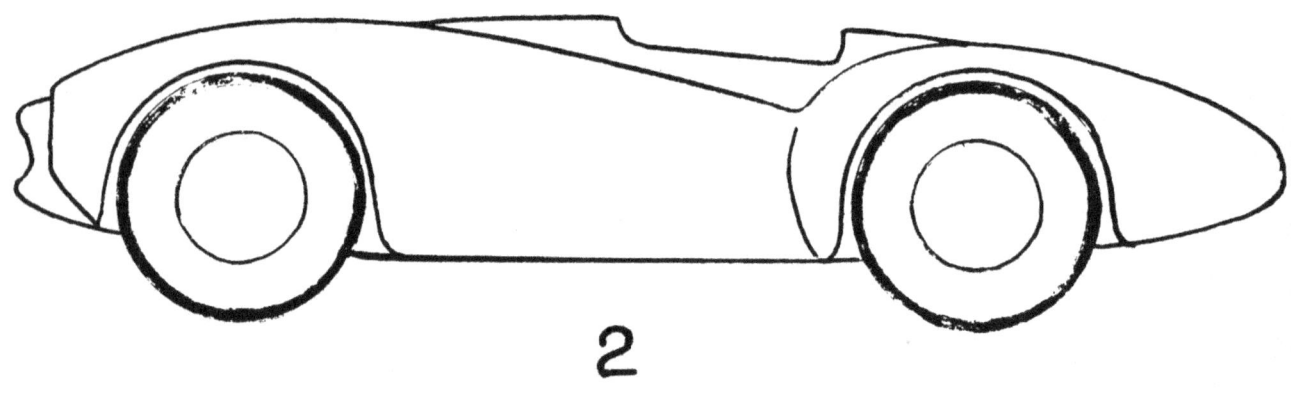

2. Clay model complete.

2

(Sketch 3)

STYLING (Cont.)

Preparation is very important. Time spent in preparation is never wasted. One hour of preparation can save four or five hours of work later on so it pays to work hard in this phase of the job. It is advisable to make at least two 1/4 scale models of your car. The first one, although it may please you, will probably not be as pleasing as the second or third one as you become more proficient with the work that you are trying to do. Also some features of the second or third model may be combined into your original model to make a final model which you will use as your prototype.

Your car should be styled to take advantage of standard items that are already being produced by the major manufacturers. For example, work out your head lights so that a standard production head light can be installed in your head light openings. Examine the method in which the light is attached to the production car fender and follow, as much as possible, the manufacturers method.

It is important to decide as early as possible what type of windshield is going to be used. If you are going to use a curved glass type of windshield such as is popular in the new cars, you will find that cutting it to your shape is extremely difficult. Curved glass tends to crack readily therefore you will have to use a standard windshield glass. If this is the case, it will be desirable to contour the coweled area of your body to conform exactly to some existing standard front windshield. Do not plan to use a back window as a front windshield as the majority of manufacturers are using Herculite which is not safety glass and will not pass the California vehicle code. When styling your car, try as hard as possible to avoid complicated curves in the door area as this compounds the problem of mounting hinges and latches.

MOCK-UP

After you are satisfied with your basic model, your next step is to translate that model up into a full sized mock-up which will serve as a basis for making the mold for your car body. Since it is very difficult to match contours of each side of the model, it is best to use one one-half of the model for your station formers. Slice the model lengthwise down the middle so that you have exactly one-half of the car. With ordinary casting plaster make a cast of one-half of the model.

Now a few simple rules to be followed when working with plaster. First, be sure that every batch is in a clean bucket. Plaster left over from a previous batch will tend to make the new batch set fast and you will not have time to use it. Second, always pour the plaster into the water, never pour the water into the plaster. Pour in slowly and smoothly to avoid lumping.

This cast will be a female mold into which a plaster cast of the model will be poured. Since the plaster female die will tend to lock if it is not properly parted, some thought should be given to how the plaster parts will be removed from the clay model. Plaster may be parted by inserting waved template portions where the mold tends to "lock-up" on the contours. The female plaster die is coated with styric acid which acts as a parting agent.

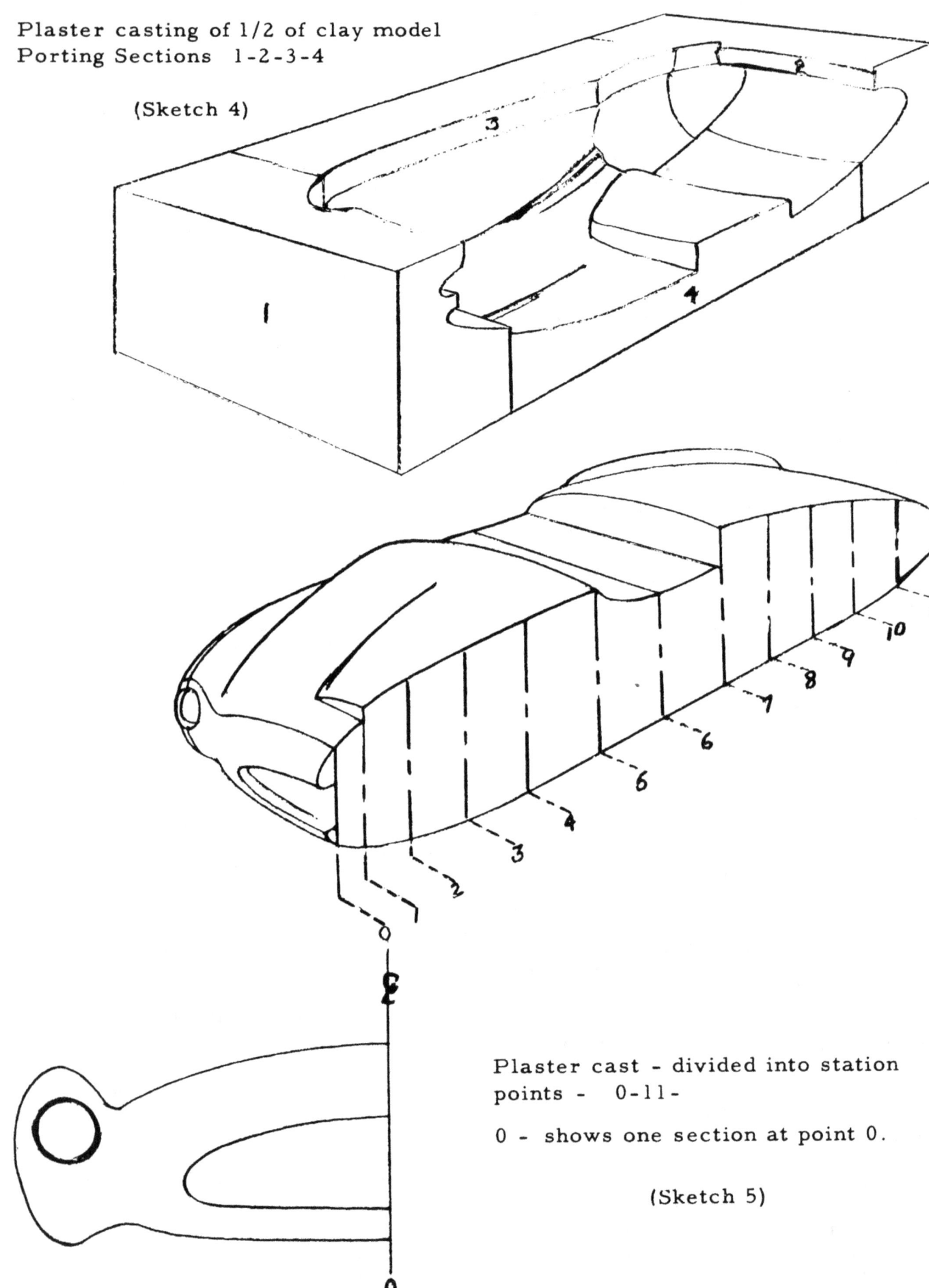

MOCK-UP (Cont.)

Then the female contour is filled with casting plaster which is mixed to about the consistency of heavy cream and allowed to set. After it is set the

(Sketch 4) See Page 3

female plaster mold may be removed from the outside and you will find that one half of your car model has been duplicated from the clay into the plaster.

The next step is to develop station formers which will act as the basic frame work for the mock-up which you are about to build. On the average 100 inch to 120 inch wheel base design, not less than twelve station formers should be used and additional station formers should be provided wherever the contours change rapidly such as in the front area near the grill and around the fenders. Station formers should be carefully selected so that all contours are clearly shown. These station formers are made by slicing up your plaster model into thin wafer like sections and blowing them up to full size. After the station points are laid out the model may be sliced in cross sections on a band saw. Station formers may be then laid on grid paper and enlarged

(Sketch 5) See Page 8

to full sized contour. A suggested method is to lay the station formers on grid paper, or underneath a sheet of cellophane which has a grid drawn on it. Photograph each former with a 35mm camera. Slides of these photographs can then be projected against plywood in full scale and the formers can be traced directly on the plywood.

(Sketch 6) See Page 10

Station formers are generally made from 3/8" plywood. Since the model was sliced in two, two of each station former must be cut out to form a left and right side. They should be cut approximately one-half inch inside the lines since the last, or outside, half inch of the car body will be built up out of plaster. The two halves of each station former are then bolted together and a hole is drilled an equal distance from the centerline in each former. This hole should be approximately three inches in diameter.

(Sketch 7) See Page 10

Now that the station formers are complete, we are ready to begin setting up the mock-up. Step Number 1 is to obtain a good location for the mock-up. If it is possible, an absolutely flat floor should be used. Also the mock-up should be made in a place where it is possible to stand away from the car and observe carefully each contour. Building of the mock-up in a one car garage usually does not give you enough room to get far enough away from your work to get a clear view of how actual lines look. Two three inch wood dowls or three inch steel tubes are placed parallel and the station formers are then strung on to them. You can check the

(Sketch 8) See Page 12

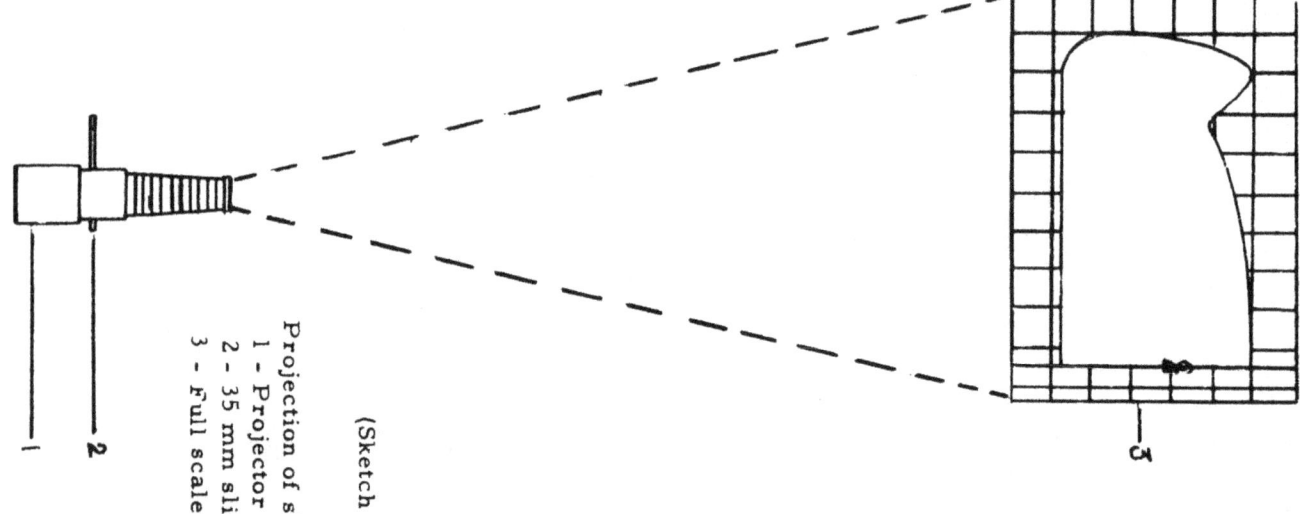

(Sketch 6)

Projection of slide -
1 - Projector
2 - 35 mm slide
3 - Full scale projection

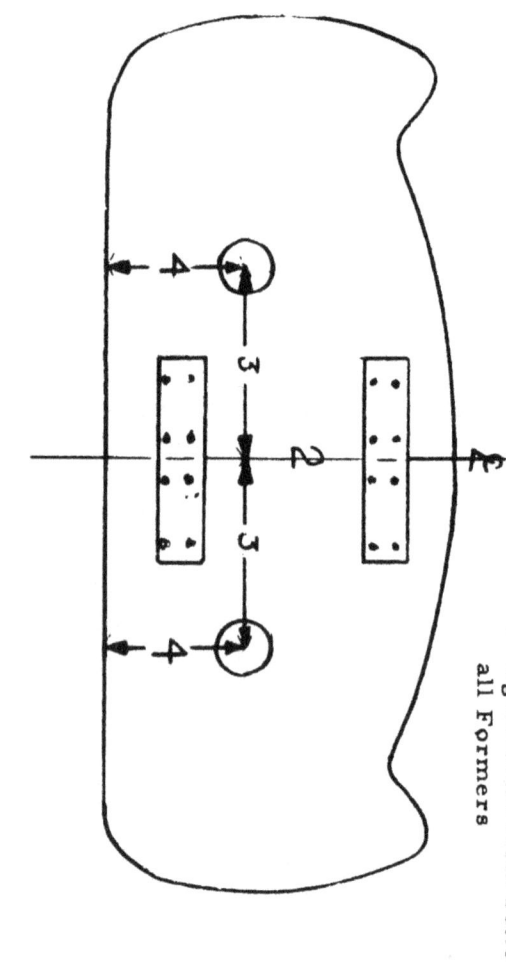

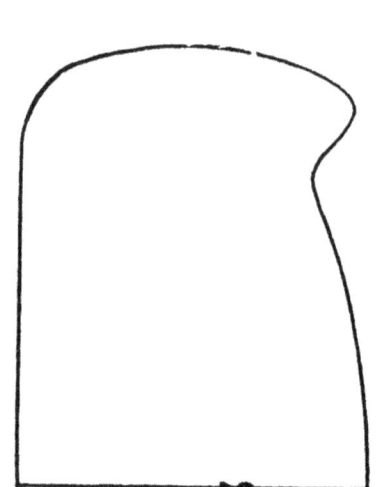

(Sketch 7)

Building of Former
1 - 1/2 Former on plywood
2 - Full Former
3 - Equidistant from center on all Formers
4 - Equidistant from bottom on all Formers

MOCK-UP (Cont.)

distance between the station formers which you made on your model. After you have them in the correct position, bolt them in place securely so that they will not move. If you have sufficient station forms you will have clear indication of your contour and there will not be great gaps to fill in. After the station formers are securely in place fine steel wire may be strung back and forth across the mold to make a mesh. In the more or less flat areas these wires will tend to create all the contour you need. String them at about two inch intervals back and forth across the length of your mock-up. Wherever the contours become too sharp to follow shape, they tend to go flat from one station former to another, fine mesh chicken wire may be tacked on to the station formers and formed by hand into the rough shape of the contour desired. After the contours are as near perfect as you can get them with chicken wire, you are ready to start working with your plaster.

Take ordinary cheese cloth and dip it into the plaster until it is thoroughly soaked. Stretch the cheese cloth tightly across the mock-up, this forms your rough sub-section upon which the finished plaster will be laid. Allow this sub-layer of plaster to dry at least six hours before applying finishing layers. You are now ready to start with the first layer of finishing plaster. Plaster will vary in hardness in accordance with the amount of water used, that is depending on whether the plaster was mixed very dry or very wet. Make all your batches consistant by weighing, if possible, the amount of plaster used in a given amount of water. You will vary the amount of plaster you put in the water depending on the hardness you wish to obtain. There is no rule of thumb but you will discover as you work with the plaster the combination which best suits your needs.

At this point the center line must be located, drawn on the plaster and established through the center of the mock-up since we are now ready to finish one side. The second layer of plaster is smoothed on and

(Sketch 9) See Page 12

then worked with an instrument called a spline which is essentially a flat metal strip which may be dragged across the surface to smooth the plaster. An excellent spline can be made from an old wood saw using the toothed edge. This gives a herring bone effect to the finish and gives a good grip for the final layers of plaster which go over it. After the second layer of plaster is set the saw may be used to scrape off the high spots whereas the absence of saw marks will clearly indicate low spots. The third layer of plaster is then applied in the low spots and splined in the same fashion.

After you are satisfied that the contours are approximately right on the third layer of plaster, a fourth layer of plaster is applied and splined with a smooth untoothed spline. Now cardboard templates of the finished

(Sketch 10) See Page 14

side of the car are made to use as a guide in matching the other side. The

(Sketch 11) See Page 14

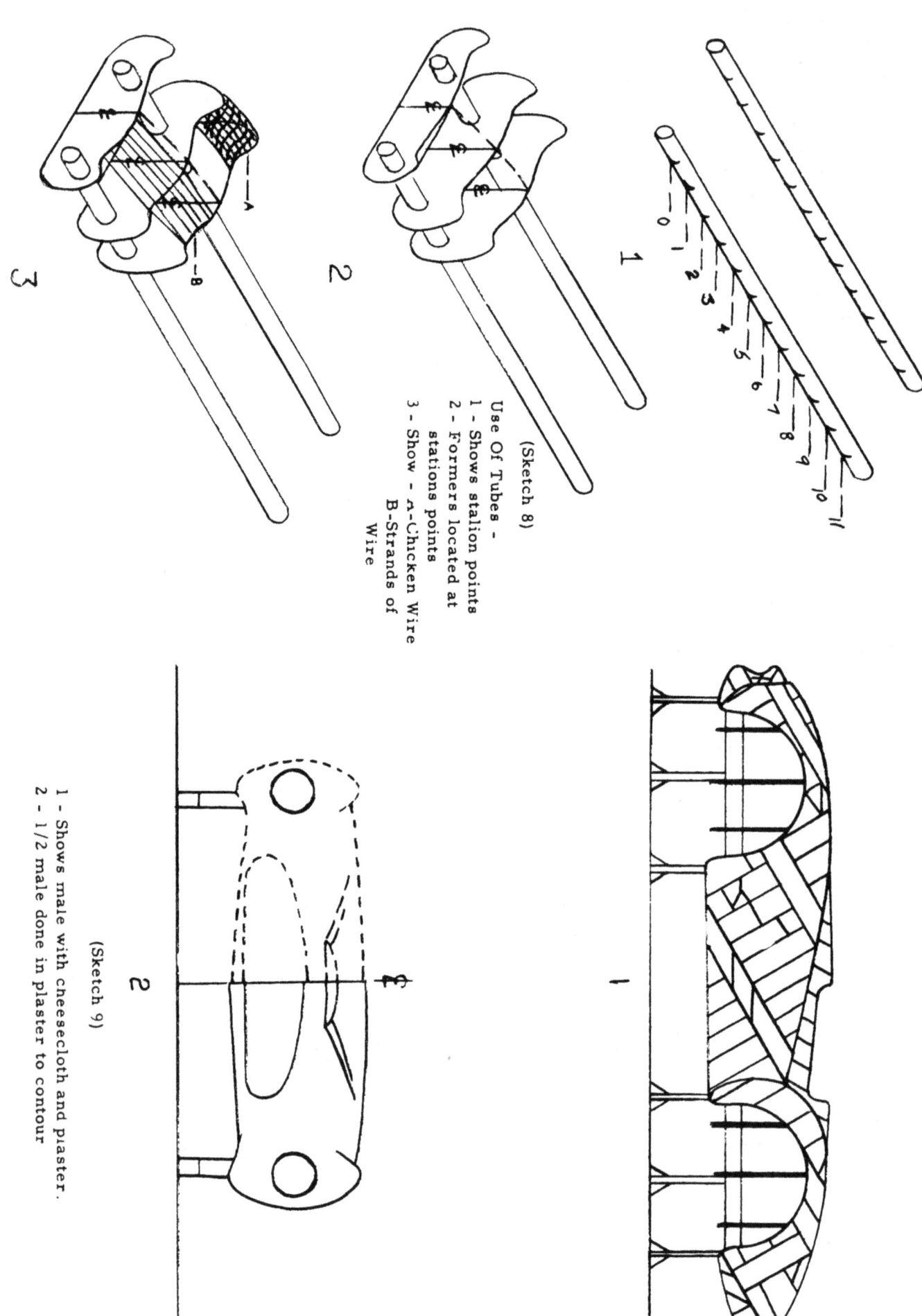

(Sketch 8)
Use Of Tubes –
1 – Shows station points
2 – Formers located at stations points
3 – Show – A-Chicken Wire
 B-Strands of Wire

(Sketch 9)
1 – Shows male with cheesecloth and plaster.
2 – 1/2 male done in plaster to contour.

MOCK-UP (Cont.)

same process again is used on the opposite side to bring it up to contours matching your finished side. After both sides of the mold have been matched and the surface is as good as can be obtained with the spline, you are ready to do your sanding.

Sanding is done with ordinary window screen nailed to a two by four block, it does not tend to load up like ordinary sandpaper. Sand with long smooth strokes to avoid creating ripples in the surface. After the sanding is completed the mock-up must be sealed before the finishing coats of primer can be added. Ordinary white shellac can be used as a sealing agent. Print on two coats. The first coat is thinned 50% with shellac thinner and allowed to dry thoroughly before the second coat of unthinned shellac is applied. After both coats have dried thoroughly, spray the mock-up with dark gray automobile lacquer primer. The dark color makes surface variations easier to spot. After the primer is dry, using the spline again, spline on ordinary automobile lacquer putty. The putty is used to fill in small indentations remaining in the surface. Putty should not be applied too thickly since it takes some time to dry. If a large area needs to be filled, add the putty in layers allowing it to dry between each application. Building the putty up in this way will prevent shrinking and cracking. After the putty is thoroughly dry, sand the mock-up with 180 grit wetordry sandpaper and water. When the putty and primer has been thoroughly sanded another coat of dark gray primer is applied to the mock-up. Let this coat dry and make a final, thorough, check of the surface for any discontinuity of the contours. If you are satisfied that the job is as good as you can make it, spray on a coat of black automobile lacquer and rub out thoroughly. This serves two purposes, first any remaining waves in the surface will be clearly highlighted by the dark paint and second, the mock-up will look very much like the finished car. If the final surface is satisfactory you are now ready to start making your mold.

It is not absolutely necessary to make a mold. The mock-up in itself may be used as a male mold and the fiberglass material may be laid up on the outside of this mock-up. With this procedure, however, the mock-up itself will be destroyed in the process of removing the body from it. Furthermore, the outside surface which is to be the surface of the car, will be extremely rough and uneven and you will have defeated the purpose of all your efforts in making a smooth surface of your mock-up. All of this roughness on the outside surface will have to be removed by subsequent sanding.

MOLD

Definitely the better method is to make a female mold from your mock-up in which you can lay up the car. This has a further advantage in that the mold is probably good for about one hundred bodies and is quite often readily resaleable to some other car builder. Even if only two or three units are anticipated, the saving in time and effort and the improved job obtained from the female mold make the extra time and expense well worth it.

(Sketch 13) See Page 16

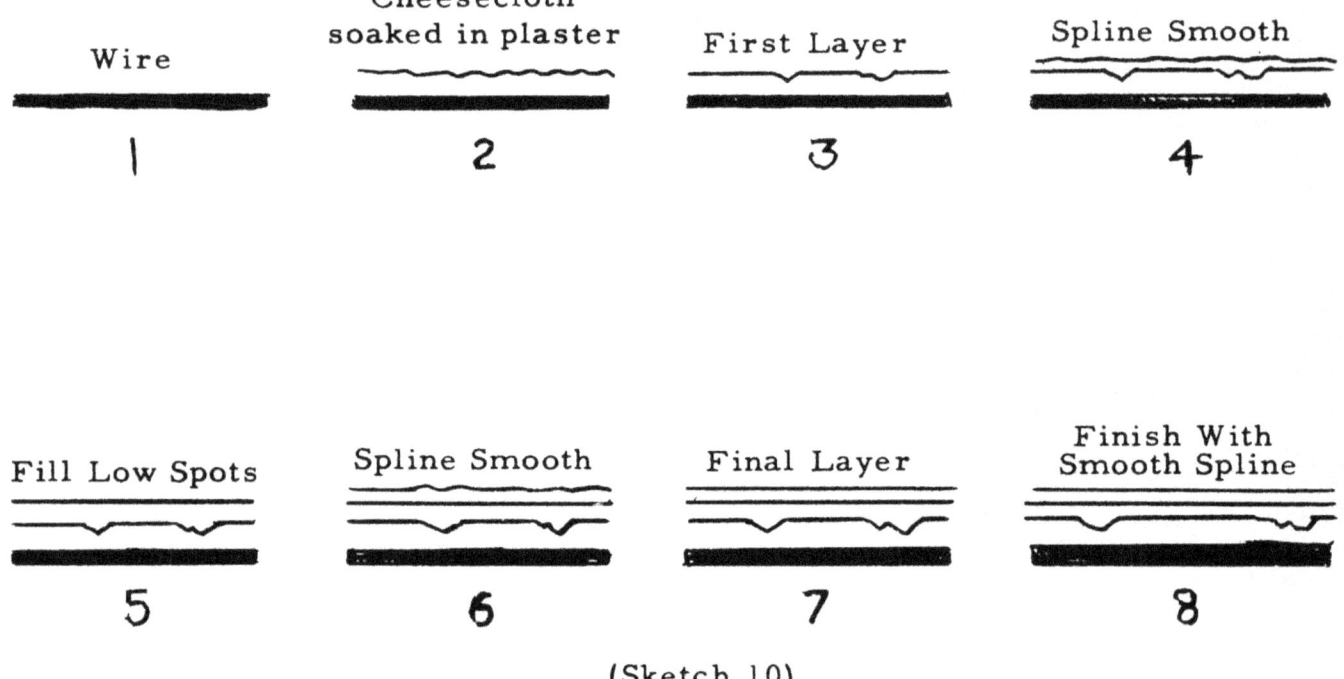

(Sketch 10)

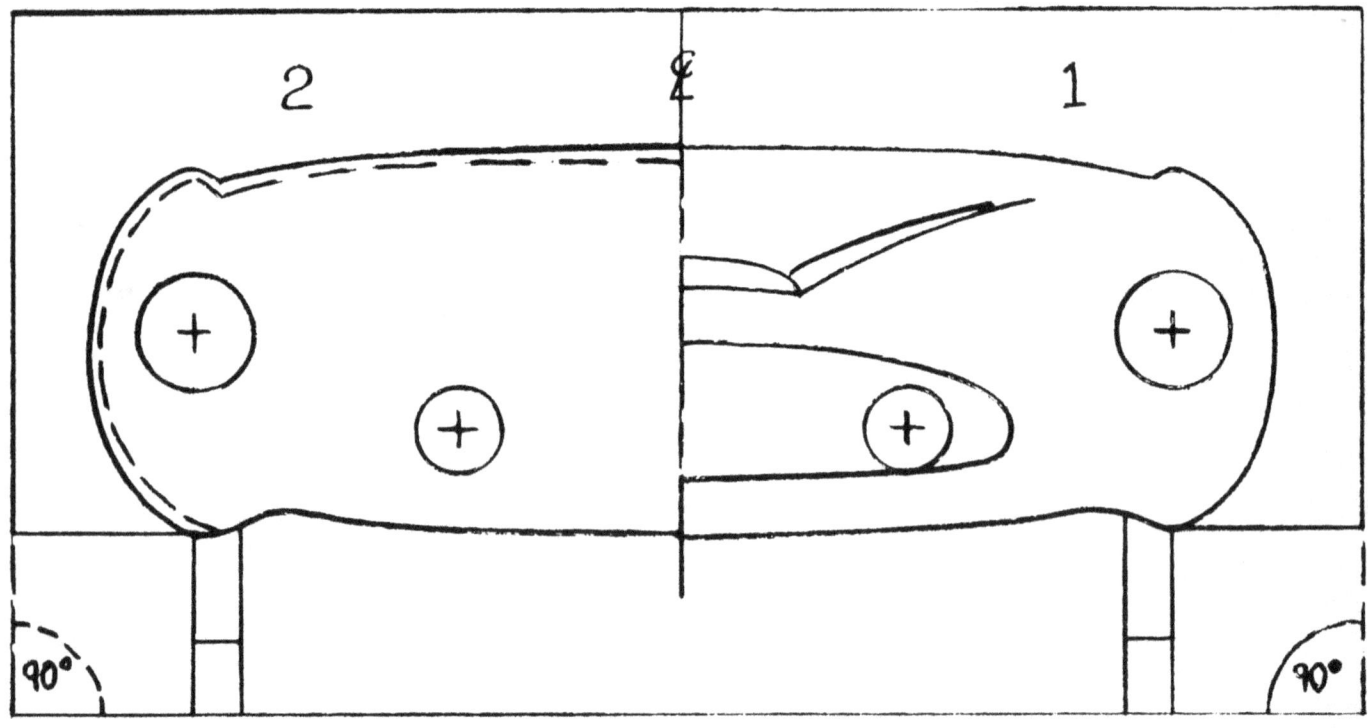

Method of Matching Both Sides -
1 - Tenplate taken from contour side.
2 - Place tenplate at same location on opposite side. Build up to tenplate with plaster.

(Sketch 11)

MOLD (Cont.)

In designing a female mold, care has to be taken in the manner of how the finished car body is going to be removed from the mold. In other words, locking curves must be avoided. If the design of the car body results in

(Sketch 14) See Page 18

locking curves on the mold, the mold must be parted in such a manner that the mold can be separated so that the finished laminate can be removed. Half of this job is already done for you since you worked out parting lines when you were removing your plaster model from your plaster mold in the original process of making the model. After you have established your parting lines, wooden or metal flanges must be devised along this parting line at right angles to the body to bolt your mold together after it is finished. If you have fairly complex locking curves, it is best to use not less than a six piece mold consisting of a hood or cowel section, a rear deck section, a tail section, a nose or grill area section and two side sections. In some cases the side section will have to be made in two pieces.

The first step in preparing your mock-up for the mold is to wax thoroughly with two or three coats of Simonize. Put it on evenly and rub it in thoroughly just as you would polish your automobile. Then a parting agent is sprayed on the mold. This will permit the fiberglass to be released from the plaster with minimum damage to the plaster. There are several good parting agents available. Spray on one coat of parting agent, allow approximately an hour for it to dry then spray on a second coat.

Since working with fiberglass and resin is a rather messy process, especially for a beginner, it is recommended that you work in an area where you have plenty of room and which is easy to clean up. The materials needed in addition to fiberglass cloth and fiberglass matte, polyester resin and catalizing agents are: 1. a couple of good paint brushes, 2, good rubber gloves and 3, about five gallons of acetone. If methyl ethyl keytone is available, it can be used in place of the acetone and is a far better cleaning agent. A work bench of about twelve feet long by four feet long by four feet wide is very handy. If you have no work bench, you can stretch out a couple of pieces of plywood sheet on saw horses. Start by laying out the top sections of the body first. Cut the cloth for your hood or cowel section so that it lays down flat over the area and goes up on your flanges and about two inches above the flanges. After your parting agent and wax is thoroughly dried, the next step is the application of a jell coat. This consists of resin which is highly catalized and is fairly hot so that it

(Sketch 15) See Page 18

will set fast. Mix up about a pint of resin, add about an ounce of catalyst and about an ounce of the accelerator.* Cover the work bench with either wax paper or cellophane to keep the resin off the work bench. Paint on your jell coat and allow it to harden. It should harden in about half an hour. Then you are ready to put on your first layer of cloth. Stretch the cloth flat on the work bench, catalize the resin, pour the resin on the cloth and using a scraper spread the resin evenly all over the cloth. One quart of resin will cover approximately two square yards. After your cloth is thoroughly saturated lay it on the mock-up. Trim the edges and work the air bubbles out of the cloth. When you have the cloth down evenly, use a

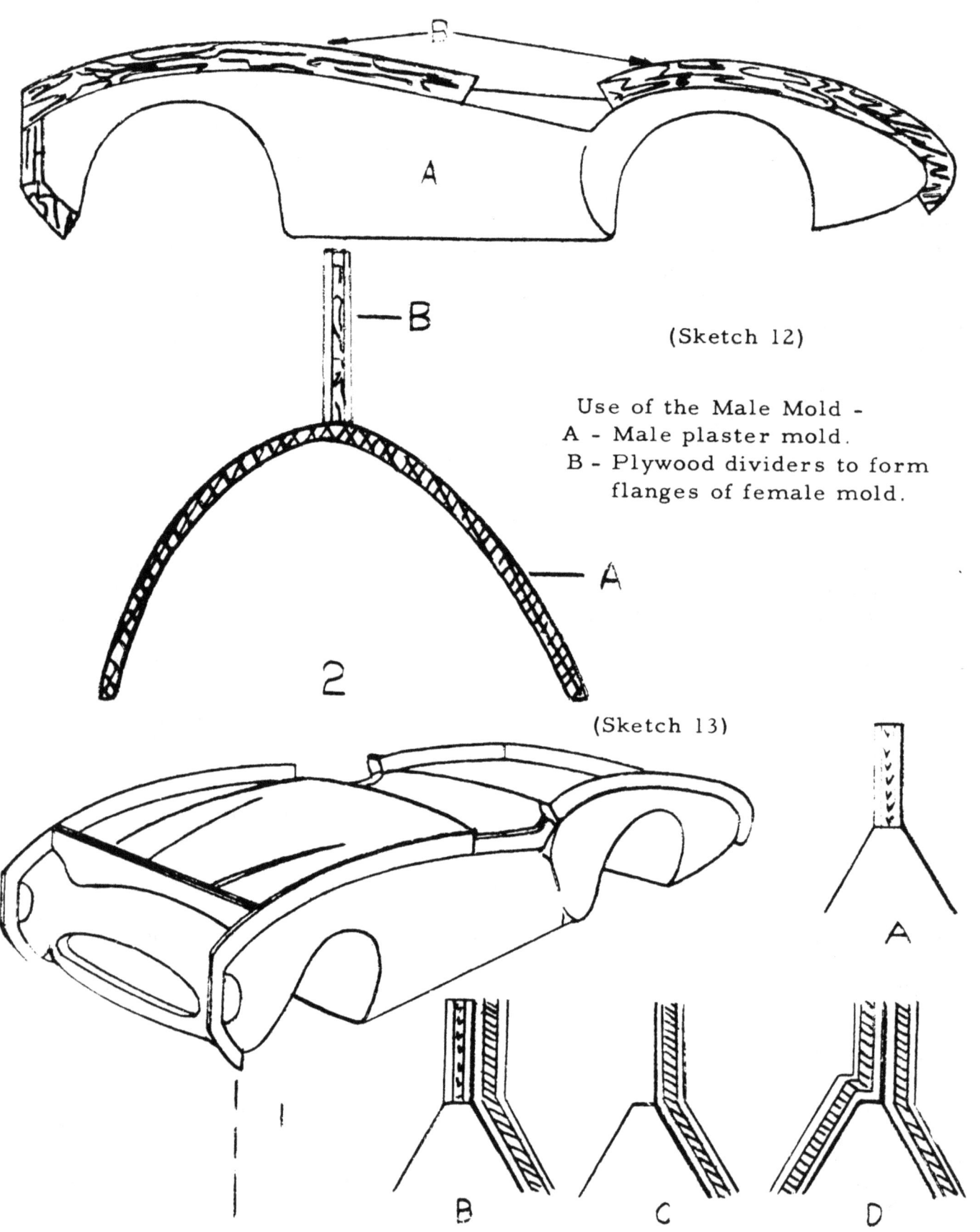

(Sketch 12)

Use of the Male Mold -
A - Male plaster mold.
B - Plywood dividers to form flanges of female mold.

(Sketch 13)

Use of the Female -
1 - Female with flanges.
    A - Waxed wood with parting agent.
    B - Lay up of laminate to form flange.
    C - Removal of wood.
    D - Parting agent and laminate for other flanges.

MOLD (Cont.)

paint brush to pick up the resin which tends to run to the low spots, paint it back upon the high spots. Continue to work the laminate until it jells. Just prior to jelling, the polyester resin will become very runny, if you are not careful the resin will run out of the cloth and cause bubbles. After the first layer of cloth is thoroughly cured lay out one cloth and one matte on the work bench and impregnate them. With an 8 to 10 ounce cloth and two ounce matte, one gallon of polyester resin will impregnate slightly over one square yard of material.

(Sketch 16) See Page 18

*Precaution, the catalyst should be mixed into the resin first and then the cobalt or accelerator is mixed in second. If the catalyst and accelerator come in contact with each other they will flame up unless they are thoroughly mixed in the resin.

Work the resin evenly into the matte and cloth. After it is thoroughly saturated, place it on top of the first layer of cured cloth with the matte against the cured lay up you have just made and the cloth on the outside. Again work the bubbles out as before. Stay with the laminate until it has jelled. You now have a sandwich construction of cloth - matte - cloth.

Next repeat the process with the rear deck section, then the tail section, then the nose section. After these four sections have been laid up the metal strips which were used to form your mold flanges may be removed so that when you lay up glass on the opposite side the fiberglass will butt against the fiberglass flange you have already made for your top section. Be sure to put parting agents and wax on your fiberglass flanges when you are butting the next section against it. Repeat this process until your mold is completed. After your mold is completely finished, trim the rough edges of the flanges down to about a height of two inches and drill holes for bolting those flanges together. Do this before the female mold is removed from the plaster mock-up as the bolt holes will be used not only to bolt the flanges together but to align your mold sections. The mold is then left on the mock-up for at least five days after it is finished to allow thorough curing and prevent any chance of warping. A partially cured fiberglass laminate, if removed from the mold, is very likely to warp since some shrinkage does occur during the curing process. Before the mold is removed from the mock-up the cradle in which the mold sections will rest must be constructed around the mold. This can best be made from steel tubing or 2" x 2" pine board which are bonded to the outside of the mold by soaking strips of fiberglass matte in polyester resin

(Sketch 17) See Page 20

and bonding the wood to the opposite side of the mold with them. Wheels or casters can be attached to this outer framework to make the mold easier to manage.

Now remove the mold from the mock-up. After your mold is removed from the mock-up and thoroughly cleaned with acetone, inspect it carefully for surface defects. There are bound to be a certain number of small pits or trapped air bubbles close to the surface. Puncture these bubbles wherever they are found and fill them with No. 506 Delux Synthetic Putty. Since this putty is a synthetic base, it will dry slowly and require about three days to become completely hard. After the putty is hardened, the surface may be sanded smooth.

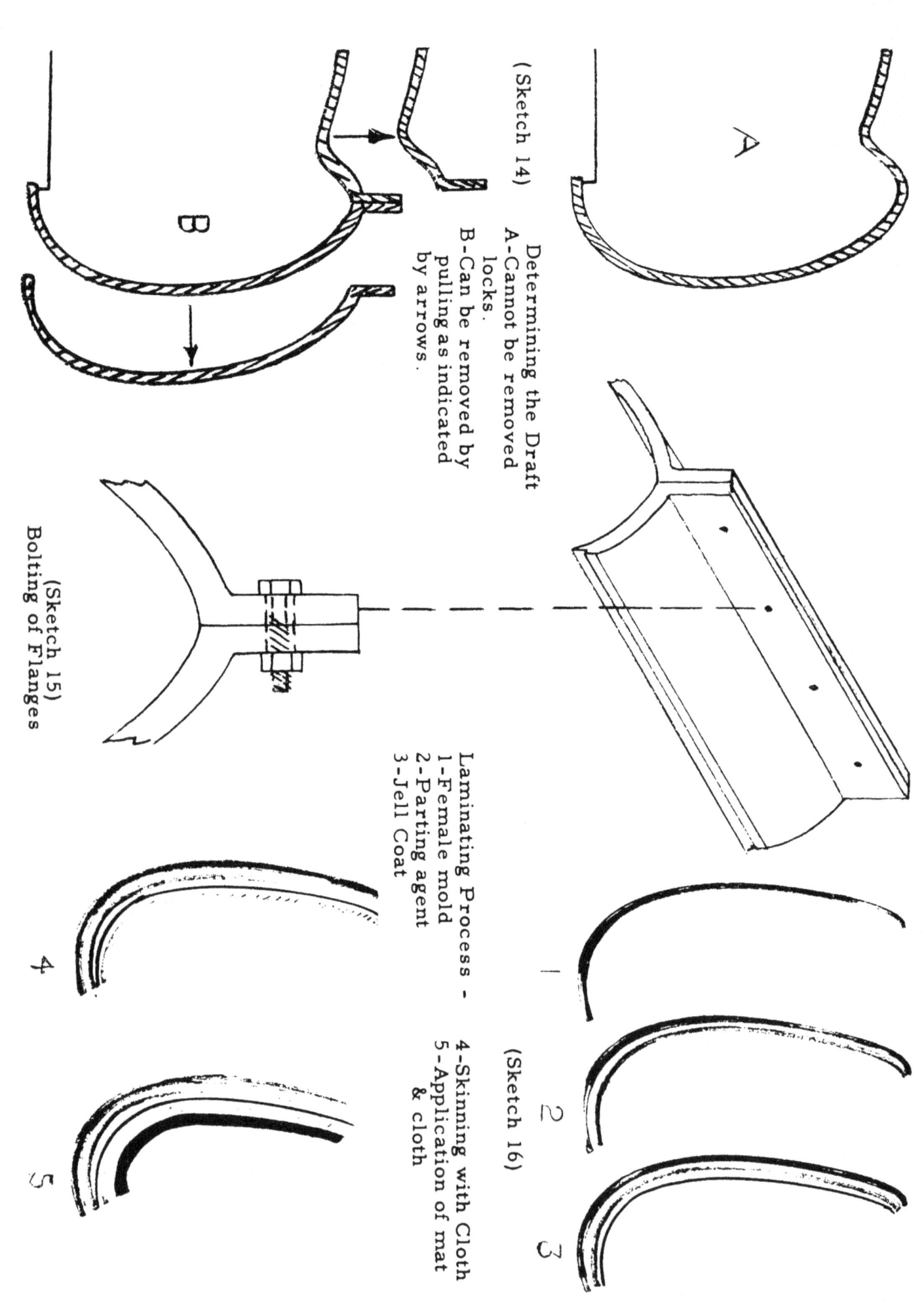

(Sketch 14) Determining the Draft locks.
A-Cannot be removed
B-Can be removed by pulling as indicated by arrows.

(Sketch 15) Bolting of Flanges

(Sketch 16)
Laminating Process –
1-Female mold
2-Parting agent
3-Jell Coat
4-Skinning with Cloth
5-Application of mat & cloth

MOLD (Cont.)

Now give the entire inside surface of the mold a light sanding with No. 180 wetordry sandpaper and water. This light sanding will remove the glaze and give the parting agent a better surface to which to stick.

The molding methods discussed in this book have dealt entirely with the free laminate or hand layup process. This is, in all probability, the only process which can be used for making of fiberglass car bodies, since the area to be covered is large and contains complex curves. However, a smaller unit such as racing car noses, tops, crash helmets and other items which are less than one square yard in material are going to be made, there are several other molding methods which are more satisfactory.

The entire field of reinforced plastics is known by another name - low pressure laminate. It is obvious that only low pressures may be used in resins in conjunction with fiberglass as any high pressures would tend to force the resin out from the glass and leave nothing but glass in its place. Therefore, only the very lowest pressures are used even when matched plate dies are designed. When we speak of low pressures we generally never mean in excess of 200 psi pressure, whereas when high pressures are mentioned, it is generally in terms of three and four thousand pounds and higher. Nature has, however, given us a method of applying a pressure to fiberglass and resin which is ideal for fabricating the material. The atmospheric pressure at sea level of 14 psi does not in any way disturb the resin from its intended purpose but makes it possible for the laminator to get rid of any air that he may have trapped in his laminate and also give good services. This combination tends to give a far stronger part. There is, however, one difficulty in fusing the molding with room temperature layups. It is primarily designed to use with a catalized resin without accelerator. After the part has been finished, bag molded and the air withdrawn making the vacuum, it is cured in an oven. By working rather quickly, and having developed a technique, this application can be done with room temperature set ups. There is definitely a short time to work and low catalization is recommended even though the cure does take a considerably longer time.

VACUUM BAG MOLDING

The vacuum bag molding method was developed by the aircraft industry in order to obtain parts of high strength without becoming involved in expensive tooling. Vacuum bags make possible a part which is about 50% stronger while at the same time using approximately one half as much resin. Furthermore, a vacuum bag makes the removal of air bubbles a relatively simple task. A vacuum molded part will contain absolutely no air bubbles if it is properly made. The method itself is relatively simple.

First, a laminate sandwich is impregnated with resin and laid in the mold in the same manner as the wet layup process. The laminate is laid on smoothly but no particular effort is made to let the air bubbles out of the laminate. Then the layup is covered with a sheet of polyvinyl alcohol or polyvinyl chloride film to a thickness of about three mils. This sheet is then sealed airtight around all edges. The vacuum tube is inserted in the bag. When the air is evacuated from the inside of the bag air pressure will

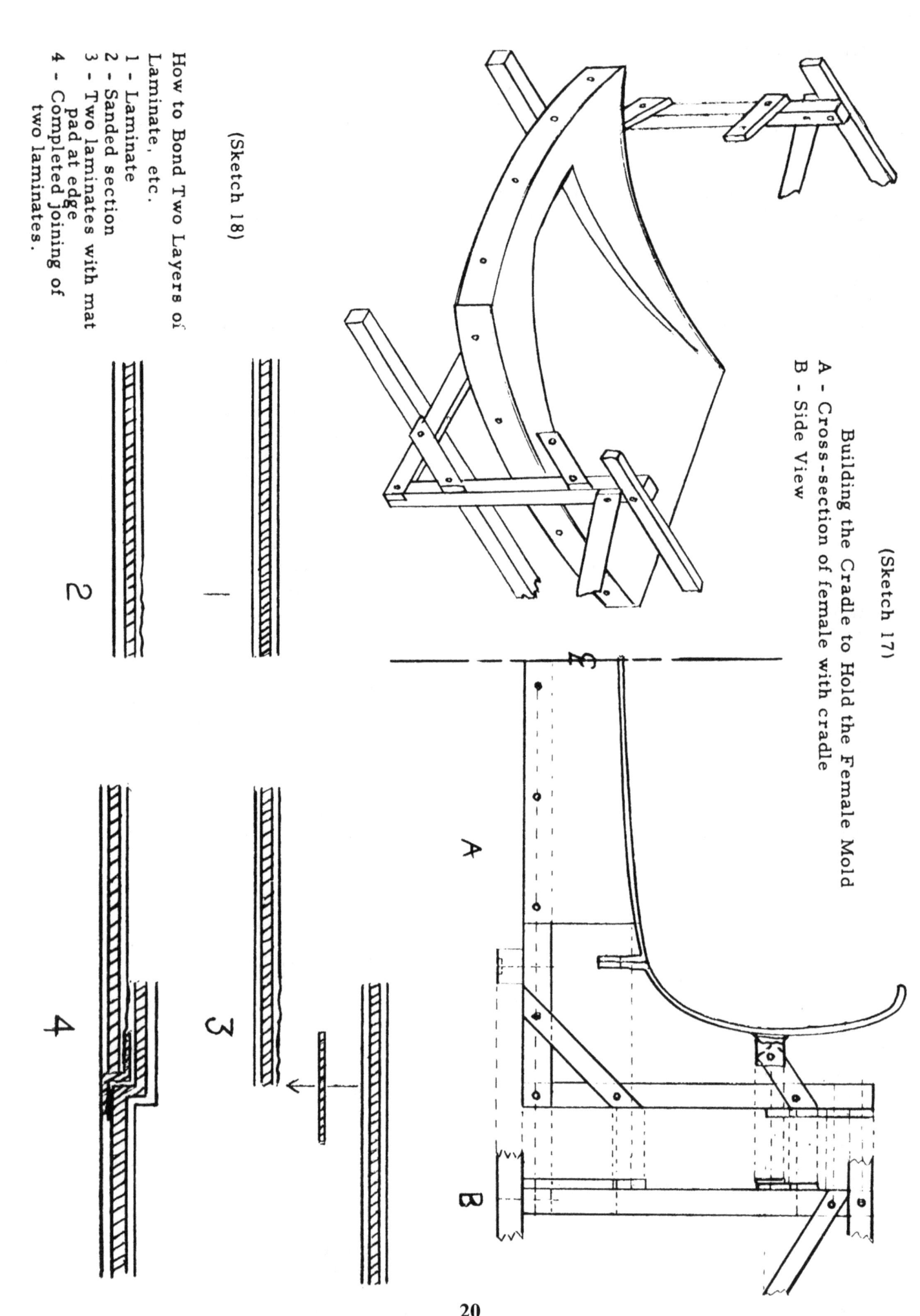

(Sketch 17)

Building the Cradle to Hold the Female Mold
A - Cross-section of female with cradle
B - Side View

(Sketch 18)

How to Bond Two Layers of Laminate, etc.
1 - Laminate
2 - Sanded section
3 - Two laminates with mat pad at edge
4 - Completed joining of two laminates.

MOLD (Cont.)

exert a force of approximately 15 psi against the laminate. This will tend to squeeze the laminate down tightly against the mold and squeeze out the excess resin. Any air bubbles left in the laminate may then be combed out with a phenolic paddle. Since no more air can enter, the problem of air bubbles returning to the laminate after it has been smoothed out is eliminated. Furthermore, since the laminate is held firmly in place, the problem of resin run off is likewise eliminated.

The vacuum bag may be sealed down by use of a gasket on a gasket table or chromate sealing compound may be used.

You will find that one of the biggest headaches in working with fiberglass laminates is getting the bubbles out of the laminate. The bubbles cause weak spots and tend to blister and rise and give an imperfect surface, getting worse as time goes by. This is particularly important in the mold. Several techniques are being used to chase bubbles out of the laminates but one of the most simple is to cover the laminate with a sheet of two mil vinylite after it has been laid on the mock-up. The vinyl at first will be very stiff but as it comes into contact with the resin it will tend to relax and either your fingers or a mold scraper can be used to push the bubbles out to the edges.

CALCERITE

There is a material recently developed known as Calcerite which can be very well substituted for fiberglass in making the female mold. Calcerite works exactly the same as plaster and is made up of a powder with an additive liquid. It is white but it can be pigmented. The main difference between plaster and Calcerite is its extreme hardness and durability. The average compressive strength of Calcerite is 15,000 pounds per square inch, and the average flexible strength is 6,000 pounds per square inch. The cost of Calcerite is a great deal less than the combination of fiberglass and resin as a material to make molds. It would not be necessary to make the original plaster mold or mock-up out of Calcerite as in this case you are not seeking durability. The time to use the Calcerite is on the female mold which you are going to take from the male mold and then the Calcerite can be used many times over in just the same fashion as you would use the fiberglass female mold.

The method of parting Calcerite from the original plaster mock-up is to seal the mock-up with a good paint lacquer such as Hyglow and then use Steric acid as a parting agent. If an extremely long life is expected from the female mold made from Calcerite, fiberglass can be used in exactly the same fashion as it is used in resin to give the part additional strength.

PREPARING THE MOLD

Before assembling the mold, the flanges of the mold should be thoroughly sprayed with parting agents since a certain amount of resin is going to run through these flanges and it is desirable to avoid the possibility of bonding the flanges together. Be sure to keep the surface of the mold free of grease. If the surface is contaminated with grease the parting agent will not stick and will have a dangerous tendency to

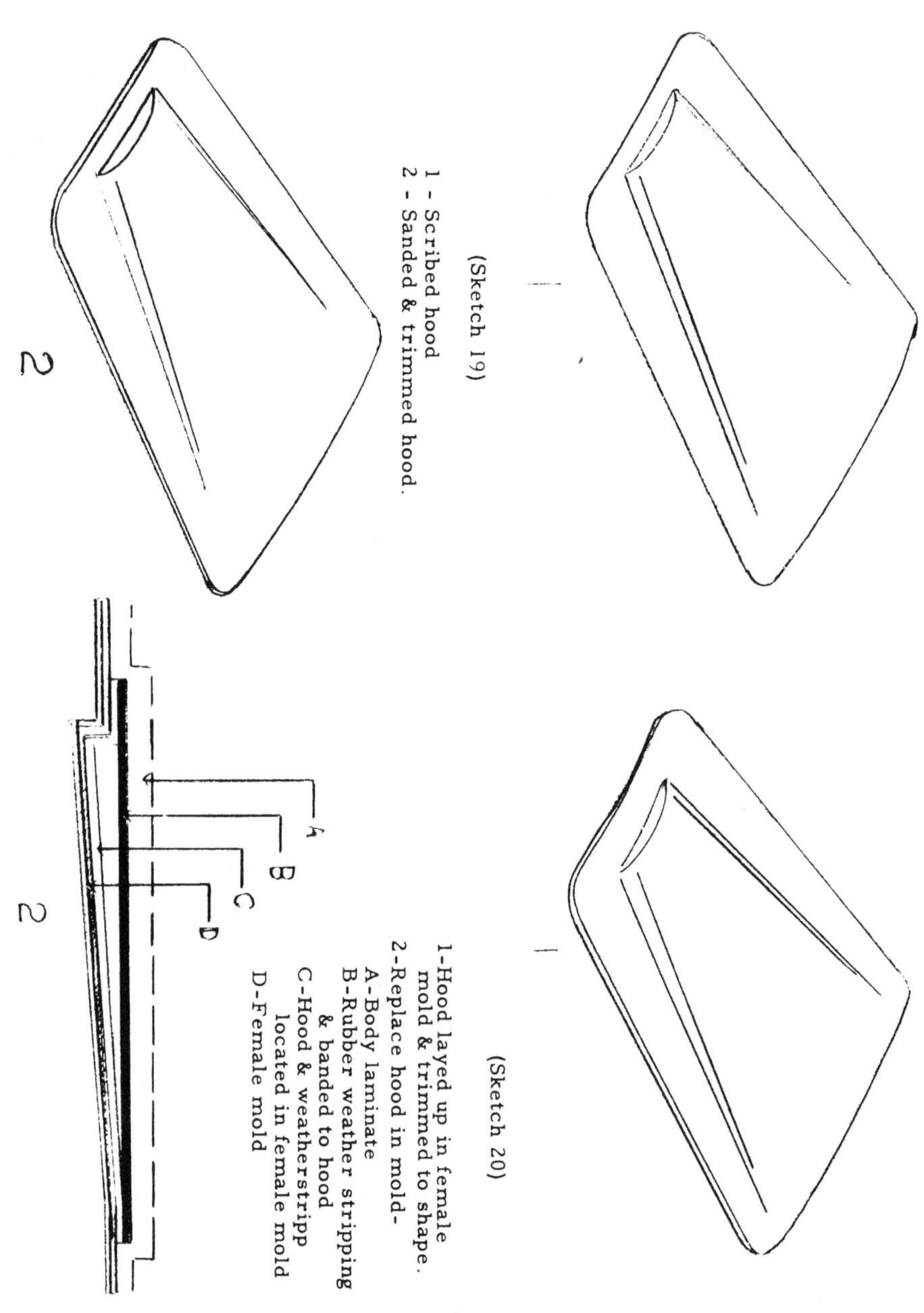

(Sketch 19)
1 - Scribed hood
2 - Sanded & trimmed hood.

(Sketch 20)
1- Hood layed up in female mold & trimmed to shape.
2- Replace hood in mold-
A- Body laminate
B- Rubber weather stripping & banded to hood
C- Hood & weatherstripp located in female mold
D- Female mold

PREPARING THE MOLD Cont.

bridge, that is, to stretch tight across the inside curves. If this occurs, slice out the bridged section and re-spray with parting agent at that point. If it still persists in bridging and the bridge area is not too large, vaseline may be used as a parting agent. Vaseline should not be used in areas greater than three inches.

The car body itself is made essentially in the same way as the female mold, with this important difference. Since the car body is to be made in one piece it will not be possible to do complete areas, therefore,

(Sketch 18) See Page 20

the sections will have to overlap each other. A very good bond can be obtained on overlapping sections, provided the overlap is thoroughly sanded before the next bond is put on it. Make your overlaps about six inches wide and sand thoroughly to expose the fibers in the cloth to the new resin going on the top before you make the overlap. Work as large a section of your car as is convenient. About one to two square yards will be found to be probably about the most easily worked.

THE LAMINATE

A great variety of methods are currently being employed in fiberglass laminating and not a great deal of agreement among any of the manufacturers as to the superiority of one formula over another. There are many of different weave patterns in fiberglass cloth and each manufacturer has developed a system which varies somewhat from the system used by others.

Special consideration involved in the construction of aircraft parts make necessary laminates that are vastly different from those found in boat construction and boat construction in turn differs from the requirements found in the construction of automobile bodies. Although the whole field of fiberglass laminating and particularly of fiberglass automobile body construction is somewhat new, the point has been reached where there is some general agreement as to the best formula or design for the fiberglass laminate. Experience has shown that a laminate sandwich composed of one layer of fiberglass cloth on each side of fiberglass matte will give sufficient strength and still remain within the financial reach of the average builder.

The cloth recommended is an open type square weave the weight of about 8 ozs. per square foot. This particular type of cloth has a great deal of bias which allows it to be pulled around complicated contours without ruffling. While fiberglass cloth is considerably stronger than fiberglass matte, cloth used by itself produces a laminate which is extremely flexible unless eight or more layers of cloth are used. Since the laminate of eight layers is far too expensive for the average home car builder, additional bulk which contributes to rigidity is gained through the use of fiberglass matte. The glass matte is made of random glass fibers which are pressed together in much the same way as felt is made. By making a sandwich laminate we have a cloth on each side of the matte. The cloth will provide the necessary strength and impact resistance while the matte will add rigidity through increased thickness. Good lami-

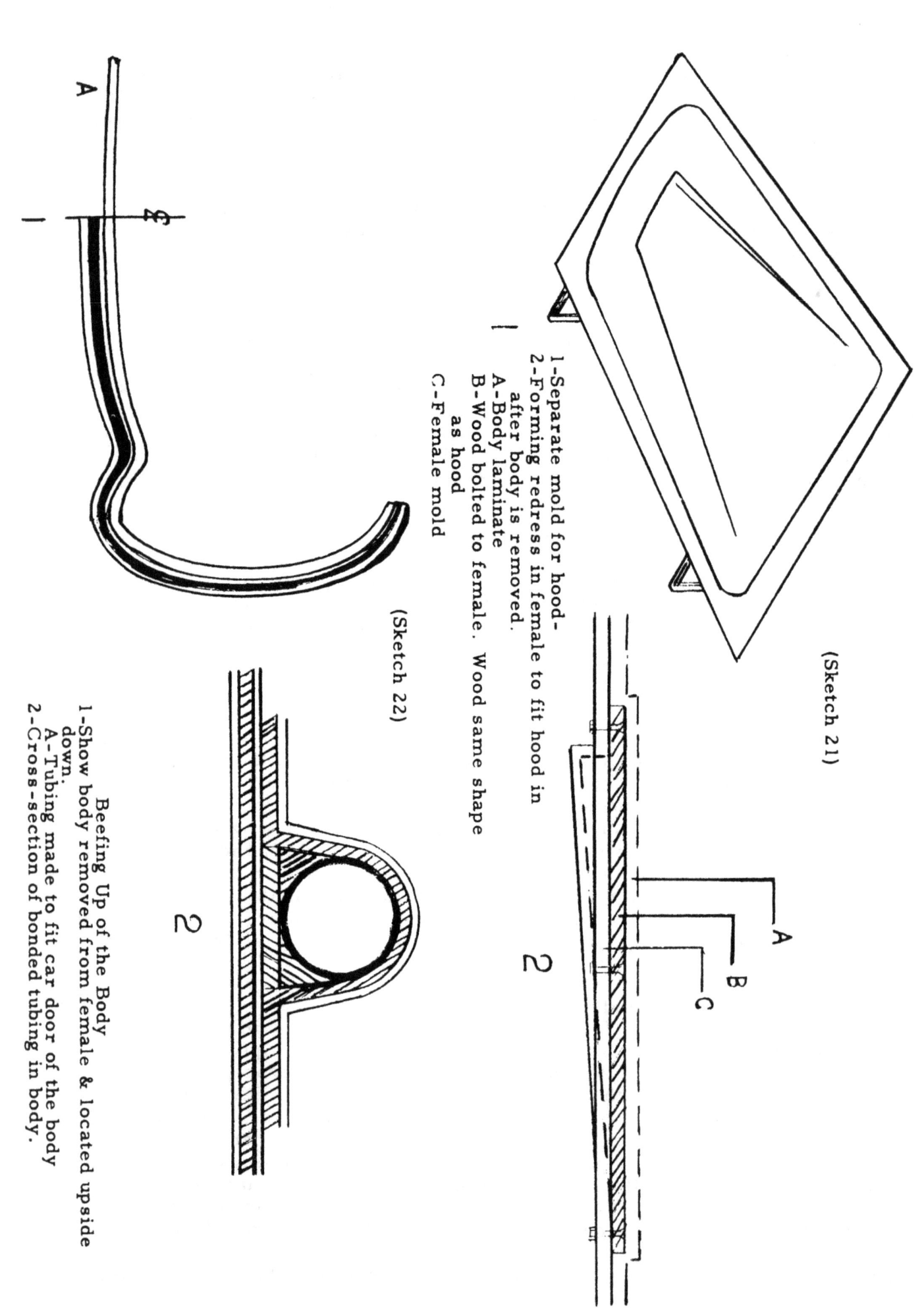

(Sketch 21)

1 - Separate mold for hood.
2 - Forming redress in female to fit hood in after body is removed.
A - Body laminate
B - Wood bolted to female. Wood same shape as hood
C - Female mold

(Sketch 22)

Beefing Up of the Body
1 - Show body removed from female & located upside down.
A - Tubing made to fit car door of the body
2 - Cross-section of bonded tubing in body.

THE LAMINATE (Cont.)

nates can be made by using an 8 oz. cloth, that is a cloth weighing approximately 8 oz. per square yard, in combination with a matte weighing 18 ozs. per square yard. The matte is generally designated by weight per square foot and is known as 2 oz. matte.

A new type of matte is now being imported from France which used together with a layer of 8 oz. cloth on either side appears to make the perfect laminate for car bodies. Known as Genin 7095, this material consists of thick bundles of fibers woven squarely together. Its great advantage is that because of its thickness only one layer need be used to attain a most adequately strong laminate. More expensive per pound than ordinary matte, the end result is a cheaper laminate by elimination of a great deal of labor. At first it may seem difficult to properly impregnate 7095 but that is more because the large bundles of glass fibers refract light in the cured laminate and this gives the impression of resin starved areas. Normal application of resin to 7095 will impregnate the material.

MAKING THE HOOD

The hood may be made in three different ways. The first and probably the most simple is to make the complete car body with all panels in one unit then remove it from the mold and cut out the hood panel with a keyhole saw. If you lay out your cutting lines carefully and use a good keyhole saw, you are assured of an excellent fit. Furthermore, if the

(Sketch 19) See Page 22

body is thoroughly cured before the hood is cut out the problem of warpage or non-matching edges is eliminated. However, with this method it is necessary to build a flange into the body to support the hood. This flange may be bonded to the body on the inside after the cut out hood has been removed. A form made of wood or stiff cardboard can be used to work as a mold to form the flange.

The second method which is very satisfactory is to make the hood first in the female mold, remove it from the mold and trim it. Then replace it in the mold and bolt it securely in the position in which it is

(Sketch 20) See Page 22

going to be. Then the layup for the body is made and the edges lapped over the hood and bolted to the bottom of the mold. In this way, the mold will exactly fit the finished body and the lip will be readily molded in. If it is desired to have a rubber weather strip between the hood and the flange, it can be glued to the hood when it is replaced in the mold. If more than one or two units is contemplated, another method is to make one hood in the female mold, then remove that hood from the mold and use it as a master to make another separate hood mold. In this case, the hood flanges can be made by bolting in a wooden former in the female mold. In this way, the hood will be made in a separate mold and the main body section will come from the mold with the hood opening and flanges for holding the hood already molded in.

(Sketch 21) See Page 24

Any one of the foregoing methods may be used to make the deck and the door sections as well.

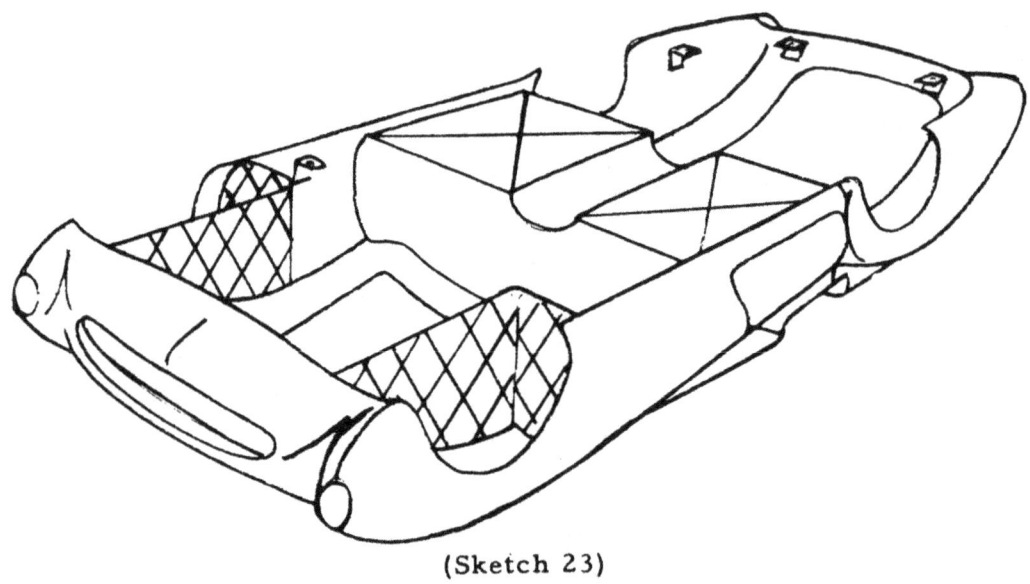

(Sketch 23)

Shows location of fender buckets, fire, wall, flood boards and mounting brackets.

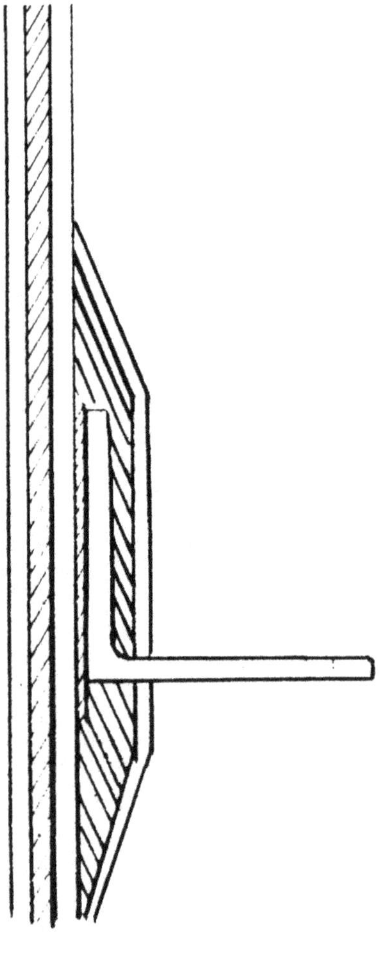

(Sketch 24)
Mounting of bracket to body

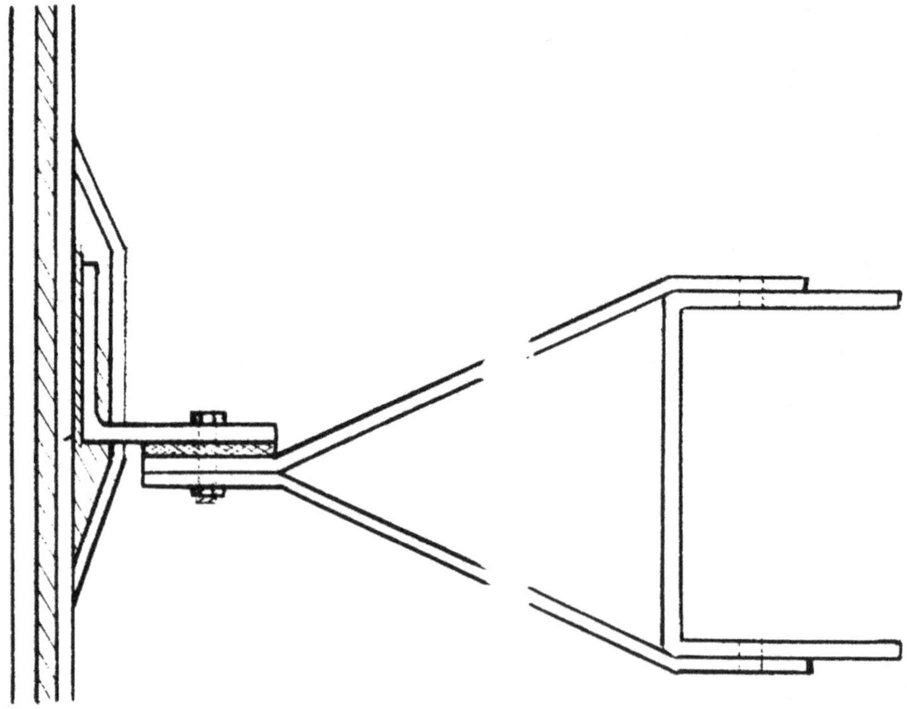

(Sketch 25)   Mounting of body to frame, mounting bracket on the rubber pad.

REMOVING THE BODY FROM THE MOLD

After the body has cured in the mold for about twenty-four hours, it may be removed. The first step in removing the body from the mold is to trim all ragged edges that are hanging out over the edge of the mold and may tend to lock, preventing removal. This may then be done with an ordinary coping saw.

The second step is to remove all bolts from the flanges. Insert wedges along the flanges at intervals of about one foot. Work them all in gradually. As the wedges are shoved further into the flanges you will hear a cracking, popping noise and you will see that the body is beginning to part from the mold. After all flanges have been parted, use screw drivers or wedges to part the lower edge of the body from the mold all the way around. After the flanges are loosened and the lower edge is loose, considerable pressure can then be exerted on the body to pop it loose from the mold the rest of the way.

CLEANING THE MOLD

If an acetate base parting agent is used, the mold may be cleaned with acetone or any MEK (methyl ethyl keytone). However, since these solvents will dissolve fiberglass, it must not be left in contact with the mold surface for more than ten minutes. If a water soluble type parting agent is used, such as Marco ML-4, the mold may be easily cleaned with steel wool and soap and water.

DOORS

Designing and building of the door molding, door jamb, inner door frame, drip molding, etc., presents quite a problem. The simplest way to handle the problem is to design the car so that it does not require doors at all. If this is not possible, there are several ways in which this problem may be handled.

The body may be made complete with the door panel included. The panel is then cut out of the body after the body is removed from the mold. We then have the problem of constructing the door sill and door jamb in the body. This may be accomplished by having a special casting fabricated to fit the cut-out of the door, and bond this casting into the body by laying strips of fiberglass laminate over the casting, extending the laminate away from the casting for a distance of three or four inches. This door jamb and door sill may also be made by built up construction from plywood.

Another system is to fabricate a mold section which contains the door jamb and door sill incorporated in the mold. If this method is used then a separate mold must be made for making the doors. When the separate mold is used it is more easy to control the thickness in the door panel. Obviously, it is desirable to have the door panel thicker than the average thickness of the body since it will receive considerably more abuse. It is suggested that the door panel be made of a laminate consisting of three layers of cloth and two layers of two ounce matte. In a compe-

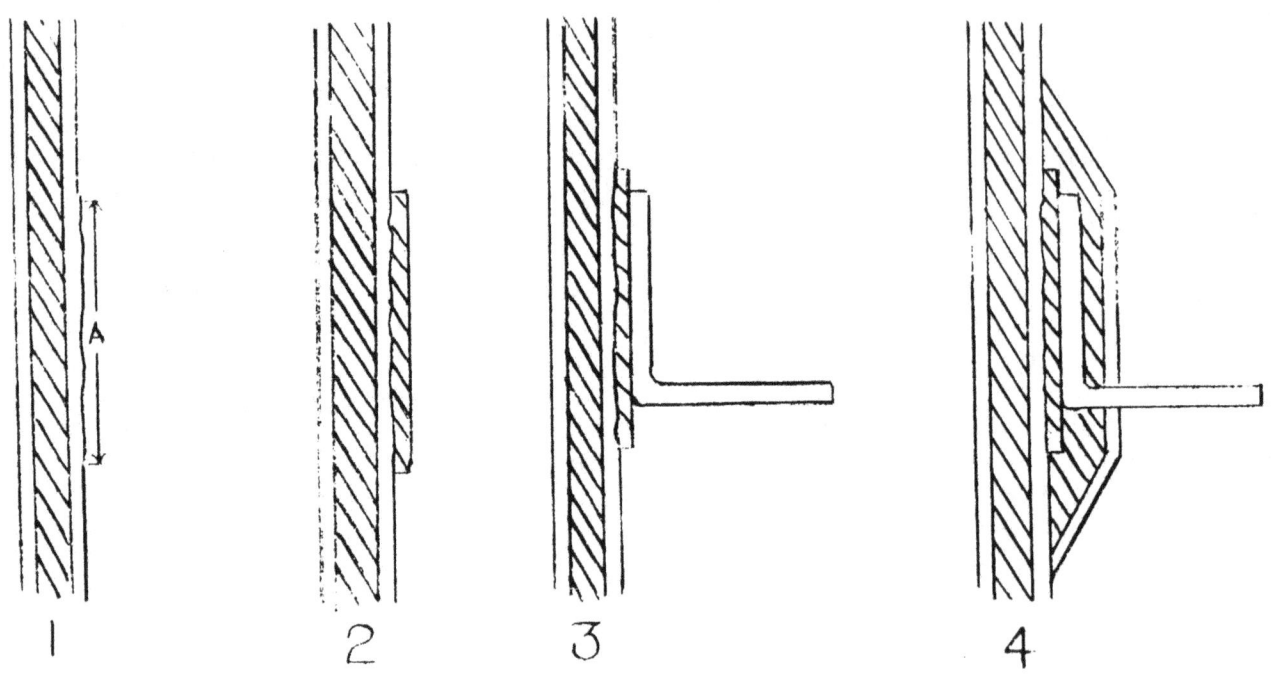

(Sketch 26) How to mound brackets.
1-Body with sanded area A
2-Body with mat pad for bracket.
3-Body with mounting bracket.
4-Body-pad bracket and laminated patch of mat and cloth.

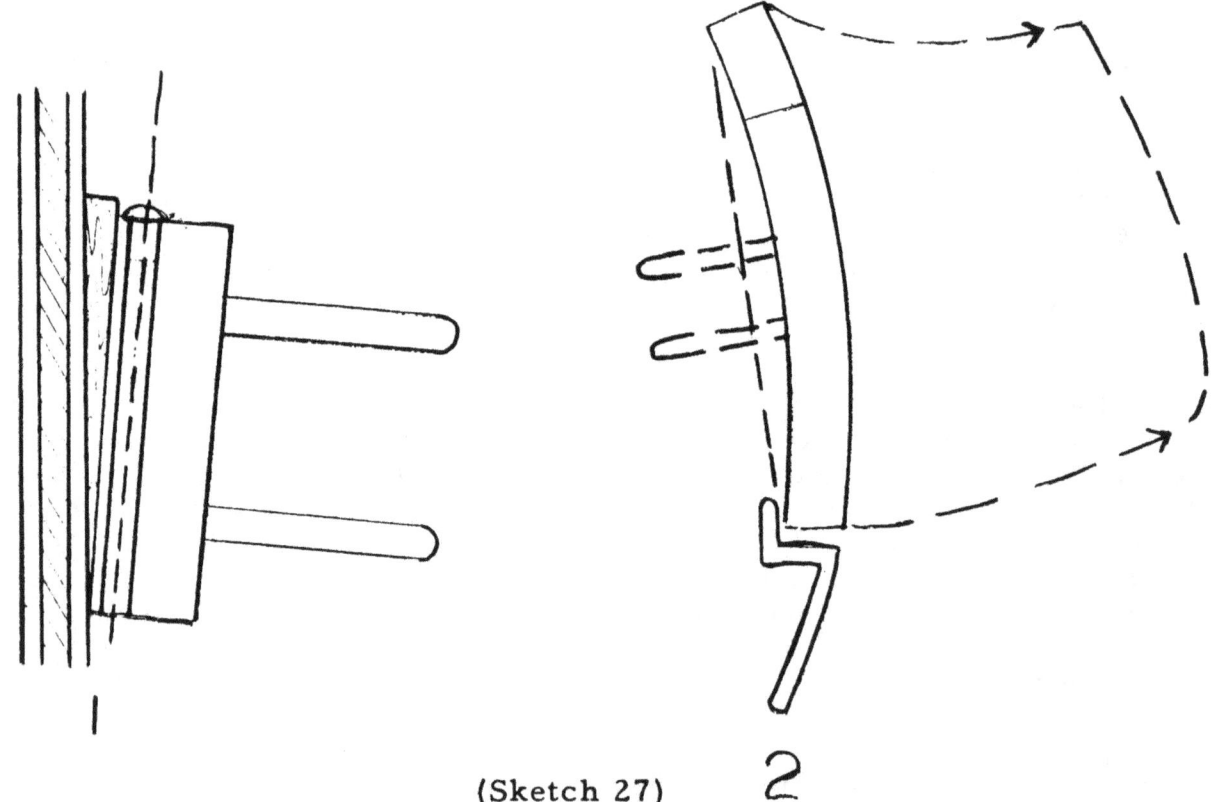

(Sketch 27)
1-Aligning of hinge pin
2-Angles door to swing out and up.

DOORS Cont.

tition body, where no trim is required, the hinge may then be laminated in directly to the side of the door panel. However, if upholstery is going to be installed in the car, then your flange must be built on the door panel to carry the upholstery. This flange may be constructed by making a simple mold or jig of stiff cardboard, clay or plaster which stands away vertically from the door panel for a distance of about two inces. When making this **inner** flange, **the door** should be bolted back in place on the body so that there is no likelihood of the door warping out of shape and not matching the body when it is finished.

"BEEFING UP"

After the car body is completed it may be found that some sections do not appear to have as much strength as may be desired. This condition can be easily remedied by laminating in "beef up" or reinforcing sections. These sections can be readily added to the inside of your car body by sanding the area thoroughly and then laying in a laminate consisting of one layer of matte with one layer of cloth on the outside. Since these laminates are on the inside of the body there is no particular advantage in flawless laminate and not a great deal of time need be spent on working out air bubbles.

SUB-STRUCTURE

It must be remembered that the fiberglass car body, when it is removed from the mold is not a complete body, it is merely a shell. An additional sub-structure must be added in order to give it rigidity.

There are two approaches to this problem. The first method is to form tubing around the inside of the body to the exact inside body contour and then weld these tubes to your chassis. Then the body is laid over the tubes. One tube should be located at the point of the fire-

(Sketch 22) See Page 24

wall, another at the backrest, one forward of the hood and one back of the opening for the rear deck. These tubes can then be bonded into the body at intervals with strips of fiberglass and the whole unit is held rigidly in place.

Brackets and other metal objects may be bonded into fiberglass quite easily by follow ng these simple steps.

First, sand the fiberglass thoroughly in an area extending about three or four inches beyond the bracket in all directions. This is done to expose the glass fibers so that the laminate which is about to be laid over the bracket will have a good bonding surface.

Second, soak a piece of 2 oz. fiberglass matte in resin and lay it against the sanded surface.

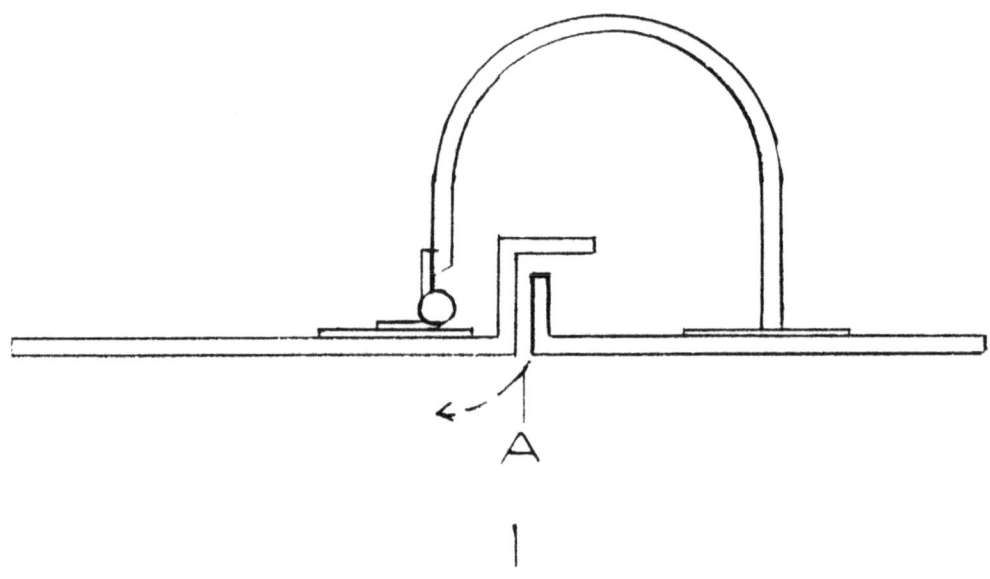

1

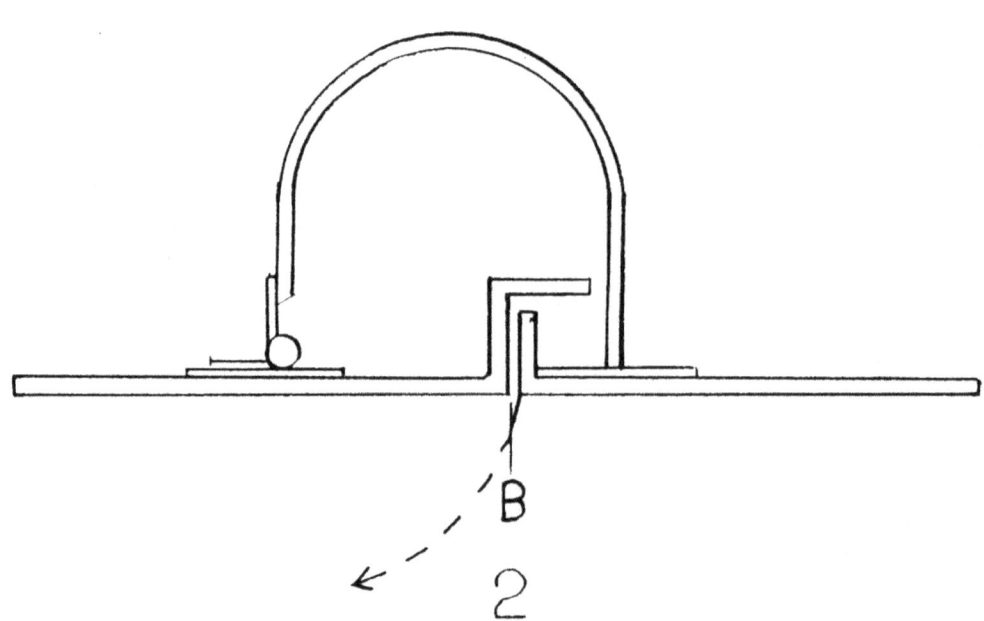

2

(Sketch 28)

Mounting of Hinges -
1 - Will not work - will lock at point A hinge located too near opening.
2 - Will work - door swings out and then arcs. Clears point B.

SUB STRUCTURE (Cont.)

Third, place the bracket against the fiberglass matte, this is done so that the bracket will conform exactly to the surface upon which it is to be imbedded.

Fourth, make a laminate consisting of one layer of cloth on each side of the 2 oz. fiberglass matte and place it over the bracket. Use plenty of material for the patch sanding it away in all directions from your bracket for a distance of at least three inches. Remember metal does not bond well to fiberglass. The metal object must be actually buried or trapped within the fiberglass laminate.

However, unless you have tube bending equipment, it is very difficult to shape the tubes even approximately to the inside contour of the body and then get them to match up exactly so that they can in turn be welded to the frame. A simpler method used by most home body builders is to incorporate a sub-structure of plywood into the car. This sub-structure consists of a firewall, seat rest, floor boards and wheel wells. For competition purposes, these units can be formed from 1/4 inch

(Sketch 23) See Page 26

plywood. If the car is going to be used as a transportation machine, it is recommended that 3/8 or 1/2 inch plywood be used. Make paper templates of the internal contours of the body at the points at which you wish to locate bulkheads, then lay out these templates on plywood, saw them out and fit them in place. Fit all bulkheads into the body then set the body on the chassis and make your finishing fits. After you are satisfied that your back rest, floor boards and firewall, etc., are located in the exact position in which they will be located permanently, anchor them in place with small strips of fiberglass laminated at intervals of about one foot. Be sure to sand fiberglass at the point where the bulkhead is going to meet the side of the body for an area of at least three inches so that these bonding patches will make a good contact. The floor board may be bolted directly to the top of the frame. Brackets running up from the side of the frame to the wheel wells will help to anchor it as well. In addition, there should be at least two or three brackets along the side,

(Sketch 24) See Page 26

two in front and two in back to hold the body in place. These brackets are generally "L" shaped or "T" shaped, approximately two inches wide, and protruding from the side of the body for a distance of two to three inches. These brackets are then bonded into the body remembering again to sand thoroughly before putting the patch over the bracket. Extend the patch away from the bracket for a distance of at least three inches in all directions so that a good contact with the car body is made. Remember the bracket must be imbedded, it can't be bonded directly. Then angle iron braces may be welded to the sides of the frame extending out to

(Sketch 25) See Page 26

SUB-STRUCTURE (Cont.)

meet brackets in the body and holes drilled to attach them together. At this point, it is best to tow the car some distance making complete turns to the right and left and checking for wheel clearance, wheel balance, etc. After you are satisfied that everything is correct, remove the body from the chassis and bond in the floor boards, firewall, back rest, fender wells, etc., with four inch strips of fiberglass laminate. Bond them in thoroughly, this will assure you of a completely rigid body.

HARDWARE

Although fiberglass is extremely strong and will stand a great deal of impact, it has poor abrasion resistant qualities. If fiberglass is allowed to rub against a metal or wood it will wear away. Anything touching fiberglass must be either bonded directly into the fiberglass so that no motion is possible or a spacer made of rubber must be incorporated so that the fiberglass is free to flex. You cannot screw or bolt hardware into fiberglass. In a short time the bolt heads will work loose and pull through leaving an ugly hole. However, it is quite simple to bond hardware into your finished body, or plan to laminate metal

(Sketch 26) See Page 28

plates into the body during its construction.

Although fiberglass laminate will not contact bond very well to metal, it can be imbedded in fiberglass in such a way that it is unable to work loose. This may be done by actually burying metal brackets beneath the sandwich of laminates. Sand the surface thoroughly for an area extending away in all directions about four inches around the spot in which you want to locate a bracket. Hold the bracket in place and lay a patch of fiberglass laminate over it. This patch should be large enough to extend away from the bracket in all directions for a distance of at least three inches. Hood and rear deck hinges may also be bonded on in this fashion. However, it is usually more satisfactory to bond in wooden or metal mounting plates for hinges and latches, since a certain amount of adjustment may be necessary. An excellent idea is to use stud plates, that is, a flat metal plate with bolts or studs welded onto it. This plate is then bonded to the body and the hinge or latch can be fastened to it with nuts. Caution should be used when mounting hinges. A great deal of thought should be given to the exact position in which a hinge is going to be mounted. Hinge geometry is not as simple as it appears to be at first glance. If the hinges are not properly mounted they may bind. If two hinges are being used, remove the hinge pins and insert a metal rod

(Sketch 27) See Page 28

in its place. Thus with one rod acting as a hinge pin for both hinges, the holes will be accurately aligned and they will work freely without binding on each other. Also the hinge pins should be located as far back from the panel as is practical. The hinge pin located close to the opening is almost certain to bind and open with great difficulty.

(Sketch 28) See Page 30

TRIMMING

After the body has been removed from the mold, you are ready to begin the finishing.

First, saw off the rough edges to the approximate trim line with a coping saw. Then finish file the edges with a hand file. If you prefer you can do this work with a portable disc sander. The disc sander will create a great deal of objectionable fiberglass dust and it is recommended that a respirator be used. Do not attempt to use a disc sander on a finished or outside surface. Fiberglass, while strong, is easily gouged by high speed sanders.

Next, remove the remaining film of parting agent. If you have used an acetate base parting agent you may be able to peal it off without effort. The parting remaining which you cannot peal or scrape off with a putty knife successfully will have to be scrubbed off with steel wool and acetone or methyl ethyl keytone. If a water soluble parting agent such as Marco ML-4 has been used, it can be scrubbed off with soap and water and steel wool.

After the body is thoroughly clean, examine it carefully for defects. You will notice that no matter how hard you have tried there will be a certain number of small pits and air bubbles. If these bubbles occur close to the surface they must be punctured because they are liable to blow out later after the paint is on the surface. Use a sharp point to puncture each bubble. Go over the car thoroughly. This job should take not less than two or three hours at the least. After you are sure you have punctured every surface bubble, sand the car lightly with No. 180 wet-or-dry sandpaper and water. After sanding, spray on one coat of automotive lacquer primer. When the lacquer has dried fill all the air bubbles with lacquer putty. If the holes are so large that they cannot be easily filled with putty, they may be filled with milled fiber instead. One-eighth inch milled fiber can be mixed with polyester resin to form a paste which may be applied to the holes with a putty knife. After the milled fiber has cured it may be filed smooth with a hand file and sanded.

FINISHING

You have now reached the most interesting phase of building fiberglass car bodies. You have completed a sound base upon which you can exercise without restraint your ingenuity and artistry for the completion of your product.

Fiberglass construction allows the maximum flexibility in the attachment of trim, accessories, upholstery and color. At the present time, most of the manufacturers of car bodies sell their products in exactly the condition that you have reached at this point. The basic reason for this is that fiberglass car bodies are so customized that heretofore few manufacturers have had the temerity to predesign the finish of the car.

FINISHING (Cont.)

One of the major Detroit car manufacturers has entered the fiberglass field and it is possible to buy a completed car of fiberglass but this, in a sense, defeats the purpose of fiberglass in auto manufacturing as it returns us to production methods and the resultant similarity. The actual finishing of your car body, therefore, presents a challenge for even though it may be basically sound, the outside appearance and its comfort round out the completion of a perfect sports car.

WINDSHIELDS

If consideration was given to the windshield when the original design was made, the problem will be greatly simplified. It is possible that you may be able to use components from some stock production automobile windshield. However, if a stock production windshield is not adaptable to your design, there are several ways in which you can fabricate your own. First, a simple screen may be formed from lucite or plexiglass. This is more than adequate on a competition type machine and is fairly satisfactory in a car intended for road use. However, plexiglass tends to scratch easily. You may find that a marine supply house will have brackets for speed boat windshields which can be fitted conveniently to your car. If neither one of these methods is satisfactory, the windshield frame can be fabricated by welding steel tubing together and having a glass cut to match.

BUMPERS

Bumpers present more of a problem in a sport car design than in the average automobile. Since a sport car is usually low to the ground the front bumper must be mounted so high that it may interfer with the intake area of the grill. Even such an expensive import as an Italian Ferrari which sells for $10,000 and up, does not come equipped with bumpers. The most satisfactory bumpers are usually fabricated from 3/4 inch steel tubing formed into a gentle contour which matches the front section or the rear section of the car. These bumpers, while not as rugged as the standard Detroit type front guard, have a pleasing appearance and are usually quite satisfactory.

DASH PANELS

It is often possible to design the dash panel so that it is an integral part of the body. In this case, the body will come from the mold with a dash panel already installed. Since this approach will usually increase the number of locking curves and therefore the number of mold sections it may be simpler to fabricate the dash board from plywood or metal after the body is removed from the mold. Little brackets bonded to the underside of the cowel can be used to hold the dash panel in place. Since the dash panel must also hold the steering column in place it should be bonded in with no less than six brackets.

PAINTING

Painting fiberglass surface is no different from painting metal or wood surfaces except that the fiberglass should be thoroughly sanded to give the surface a slight roughness for the paint to attach itself. In some

PAINTING (Cont.)

cases, the necessity for painting at all can be eliminated by mixing pigment into the resin. Color pigments are obtainable suspended in various carriers. Some of these are so concentrated that 2% is used while others are suspended in less volume of pigment for the carrier and therefore greater percentages are used. The percentage will run from 2 to 10 percent. Here a note of caution must be added in that some of the colors available today are suspended in carriers which will inhibit cures. Others actually accelerate the cure. If these colors are used, caution must be exercised in establishing the curing cycle. Definitely samples must be made in advance to establish the exact curing time based upon the percentage of color added to the resin. One manufacturer of color pigments actually suspends the color in resin. Here the carrier is absolutely compatible with the resin you are using and there is no problem with the curing cycle.

FINISHING - UPHOLSTERY

The upholstery in your car will probably be done by a specialist and it is his headache. However, he may need some assistance from you. Thin strips of wood should be bonded to the edges of the doors and cowel areas so that upholstery may be tacked to it. A fairly good grade of wood should be used for this to prevent the possibility of screws or tacks working loose. If you desire a leather trim around the edges of the cockpit it can be done simply by wrapping and gluing leather or plastic upholstering material around a rubber tube which is sliced and then inserted along the edge of the cockpit and glued in place with trim cement.

GRILLS

The construction of the grill is one portion of the car in which you may express a great deal of individuality. Grill stylings are almost unlimited in variation. Grills can be fabricated from almost anything, tubes, bars, sheets, etc. The brilliant success of the Ferrari automobiles has recently popularized the ice box tray type of grill. This grill can easily be fabricated by cutting matches in metal strips and fitting them together much in the same way as an egg crate is assembled. If you prefer thin vertical or horizontal bars, grills of this type can easily be fabricated from ice box shelves such as the type found in large deep freeze units. These shelves come already chromed and in some cases require very little adaptation to make them into an excellent grill.

If you prefer a grill of complete originality of your own design, the problem of casting is not quite so difficult as it might appear. A full scale model of your proposed grill can be fabricated from balsa wood and a single casting can be made by any foundry for a cost of roughly $1.25 per pound.

FINISHING - GRILLS

When designing this grill be sure and take into consideration the factor of metal shrinkage. In the case of aluminum this is 5/32 shringage per foot.

FINISHING GRILLS, (Cont.)

If the foregoing method seems too complex, grill components from stock production automobiles may be combined in a variety of ways to create a very pleasing effect.

MATERIALS NEEDED FOR BUILDING A FIBERGLASS CAR

THE MOLD

If the mold is to be built of wood, chicken wire and plaster, these products may be all purchased locally.

If Calcerite is selected, about 200 pounds will be required. In a 200 pound drum this material costs $.50 per pound including 32 pounds of catalyst ZN-1.

If the mold is to be made of fiberglass, it should be constructed of two layers of glass cloth (approximately 40 yards per layer) with ample allowance for reinforcing with thickness built up with matte (about 20 pounds). The glass cloth is available at $1.30 per yard, 38" wide. The matte can be purchased for $.50 per pound in easy-to-use assorted sizes.

From 20 to 25 gallons of resin will be needed to make the mold. Resin - $24.00 per 5 Gal.; Catalyst - 8 lb. Jar - $20.00; Accelerator - $4.70 per Gal.

CAR BODY

If the car body is to be made of the conventional laminate of fiberglass - matte - fiberglass, approximately the same amount of material will be needed as in the making of the mold.

If the alternate method is used combining Textiglass 7095 with woven glass cloth, about 20 yards of Textiglass and 40 yards of cloth will be necessary.

A little less than 2 gallons of ML-4 parting agent will be required in the fabrication of each car body.

From 15 to 20 gallons of resin will be required to make each car body.

The quantities suggested above are only for the purpose of guidance.

Actually it is difficult to recommend that one person build a single fiberglass car body for himself. The mold is a tool and tooling costs should be amertized over a certain number of units. The actual fiberglass car body should cost about $200.00 but it must be laid up on a mold which will cost somewhere near $500.00 to $600.00

CAR BODY (Cont.)

The first approach to this is to determine to build a certain number of nodies from the mold thatlyou construct and sell them for the cost of your material, labor and a portion of the mold cost applied to each body. If you decide to do this over only ten cars, you can reduce the cost of the mold for a very slight portion of the cost of each fiberglass car body and can probably come out of the deal with your own fiberglass car costing nothing and even a profit on the time which you have spent.

Another approach which involved no risk in the matter of the getting together several other men who are adept with their hands and to device the cost of the materials and the labor between the group so that each individual contributes and ends up with a car. Here again you will find that the total cost of each car body will be within everyone's reach. It has been reported that clubs formed for fiberglass car building are faced with an added material cost as varying amounts of beer are consumed on the jobs.

Each car body builder will know the exact dimensions of his own car. In the beginning it would be well to allow an extra 20% above the actual measurements for scrap and waste. This allowance has been made in the above estimates and will probably decrease as more car bodies are made due to the improvements of technique through gained experience.

All of the materials listed above are available for immediate shipments from Allied Products Engineering Corporation, 4707 Crenshaw Blvd., Los Angeles 43, California, (AXminister 3-7189). Shipment is made by truck line, freight collect, to any point in the United States. Business firms will be shipped C.O.D. or on an open account basis after credit has been established.

Individuals, when placing their orders, should send checks or money orders

1954 Advertisement

1954 Brochure

IT'S A BODY BY VICTRESS . . .

of course

The famous Victress S1-A, world's fastest sport car body (203 mph at Bonneville!), is offered at a remarkable price! Built of sandwich laminate fiberglass to fit 99" wheelbase, it's only $595.00 plus tax, F.O.B. North Hollywood, California.

The new Victress S-4 sport body—fits Chevrolet, Ford and Plymouth chassis without modification—is offered at $695.00 plus tax, F.O.B. North Hollywood.

Send 25c in coin today for Victress Catalog and construction details of all Victress bodies. Address Department 7.

Victress MANUFACTURING CO.

11823 Sherman Way, North Hollywood, Calif.

THE VICTRESS S1-A

The S1-A, America's fastest sports car body, was not the result of accidental discovery. The design—the first auto body ever built with an eye to combining sports car looks with streamliner aerodynamics—was the culmination of two years of research and engineering.

Wind tunnel tests gave laboratory evidence that the Victress S1-A was going to be the hottest thing on sports car wheels, but it remained for the Guy Mabee Special to prove this in the field.

At Bonneville, during the 1953 Nationals, Joe Mabee piloted the Special—with body by Victress—on a blistering two-way trip through the timing lights. The speed attained was a sizzling 203.105 MPH! Thus, without doubt, the Victress S1-A is America's fastest sports car body.

The streamlining and performance of this body, designed primarily for street operation, has given it the nickname of the "Streetliner."

Built by the sandwich laminate method (the strongest type of fiberglass construction), the S1-A is designed to fit a 99" wheelbase chassis. The chassis of any popular American car can be easily adapted to this wheelbase dimension, or an inexpensive ready-made chassis can be purchased from the Victress Company. In either case, the weight and lowering modifications give the resulting car added roadability and the handling characteristics of some of the finest European sports cars.

The modifications to standard frames can be accomplished by any blacksmith at a cost under $100. The necessary drive shaft modification can be done by any machine shop for $15 to $25. The body is mounted to the frame by easily installed angle brackets, and no phase of the work offers difficulties. Any person can, with a minimum of tools and know-how, do the work himself.

A wide variety of power plants have been used in cars constructed with Victress bodies, and any power plant is suitable.

World's Fastest Sports Car Body! That's the title earned by the S1-A at Bonneville in 1953 when a speed of over 203 MPH was reached by a car using the Victress S1-A body! With lines approaching the streamliner class, the S1-A is truly a "stunning" performer.

THE VICTRESS S-4

The goal of building a fiberglass sport body to fit ANY of the popular priced American frames presented many problems. Wheelbases vary from 110" to 116"; suspension systems and motor mountings also vary considerably in the Fords, Chevrolets and Plymouths from 1940 to date.

These problems seemed almost insurmountable, but, by constant trial and error, fitting and re-fitting and dimensioning hundreds of tolerances, the basic proportions of the S-4 were developed. This phase saw the building of four scale models and the expenditure of approximately 1000 man hours.

After the basic dimensions had been established, the actual job of designing a clean-lined, aerodynamically stable and artistically pleasing body was turned over to the Victress industrial design group. Two thousand man hours later, the design was finished.

The final result, the Victress S-4, was well worth the effort. Its crisp lines and low silhouette are greeted with admiring glances everywhere it is driven.

Its low weight/power ratio (the S-4 body is approximately 1000 pounds lighter than the stock body) gives it truly, stunning performance using a purely stock engine.

An ingenious rear fender well design allows it to fit any frame in the 112" to 116" wheelbase range without alteration to the stock member. In all, the only running gear alterations suggested by the Victress Company are those involved in lowering the frame-to-ground distance. The lowering process takes fullest advantage of the S-4's sweeping lines, and can be accomplished easily by any of the normal lowering methods such as use of lowering blocks, long shackles or reversing or torching springs.

Any auto shop can do this work for a very small amount, and the job of mounting the lightweight laminate body (weighs less than 200 pounds yet is as strong as steel!) is easily accomplished by anyone.

Designed to fit stock '40 to '48 Ford, Chevrolet or Plymouth frames with little or no alteration, the S-4 Victress body can be installed by anyone. Clean sweeping lines put it in the futuristic Dream Car class, yet, using it, you can build your own Dream car for approximately $1,000.00!

THE VICTRESS S1-A

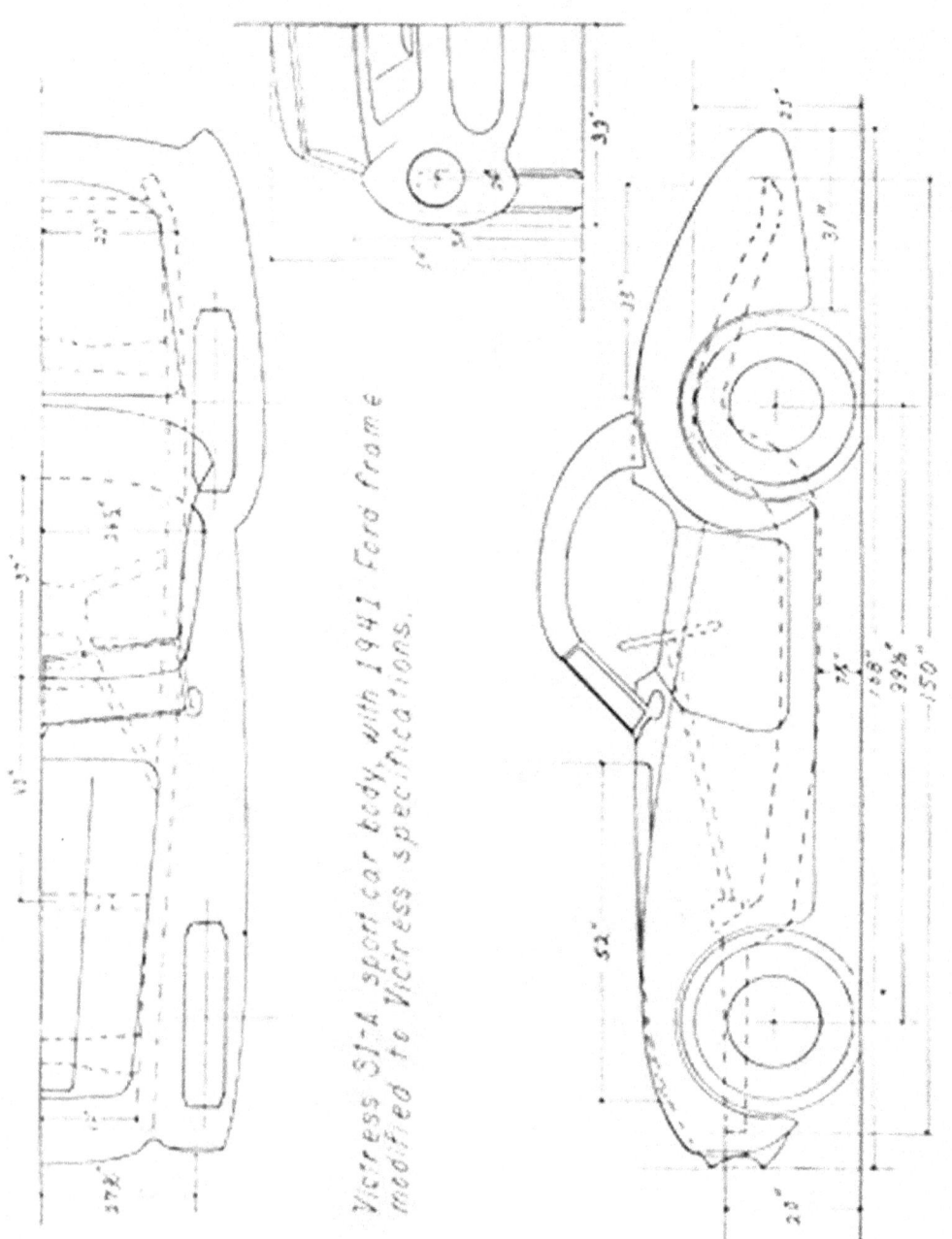

Engineering drawing of the Victress S1-A Body, showing important dimensions. The frame, shown by dotted lines in plan and side views, is a 1941 Ford frame modified to Victress specifications. You can have this work done on any frame, or you can purchase modified frames directly from Victress.

THE VICTRESS S-4

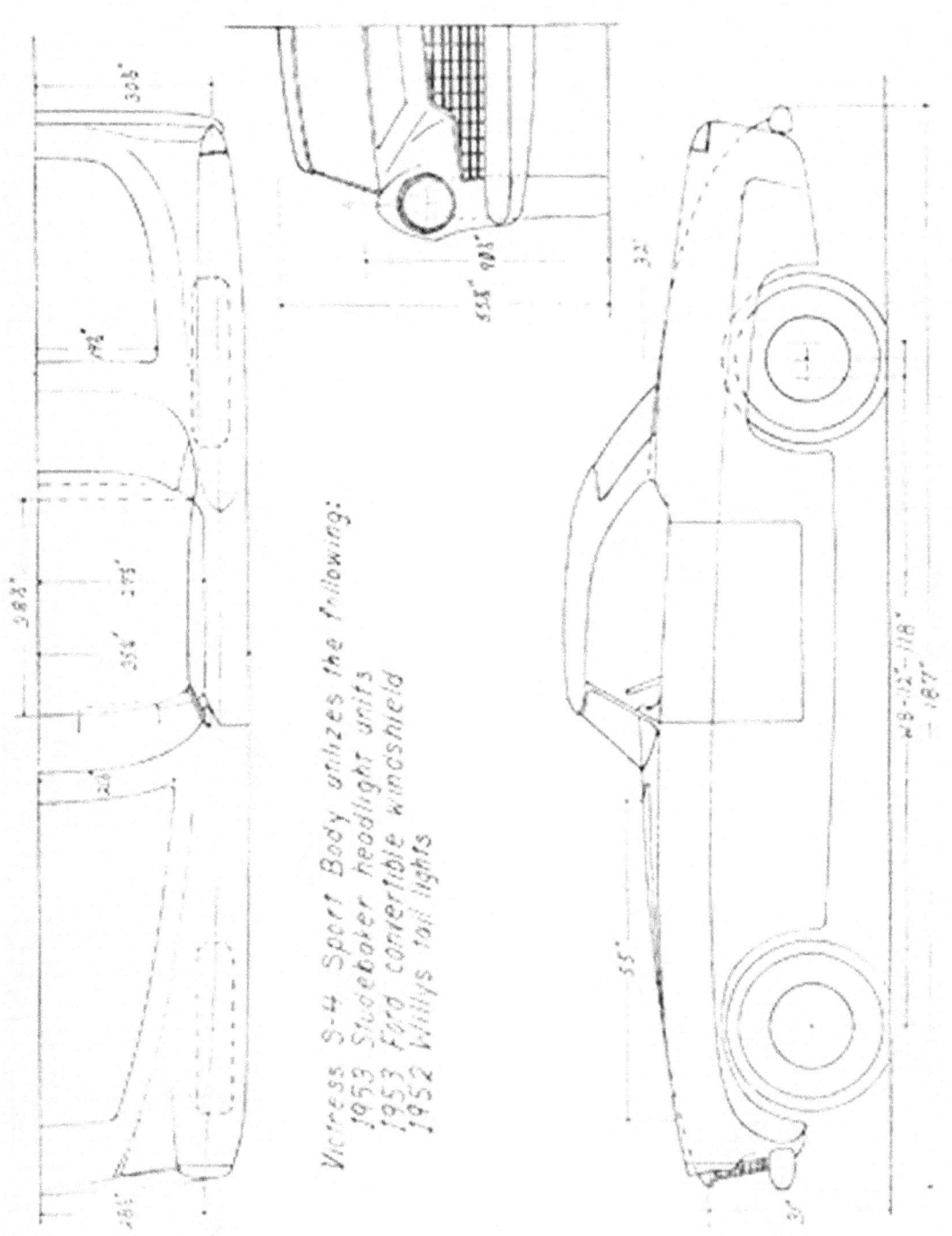

These drawings show some of the dimensions of the Victress S-4. Headlights represented here are 1953 Studebaker units, tail lights are 1952 Willys, and the suggested windshield is from a 1953 Ford convertible. Windshield frame is included with all finished kits.

CONSTRUCTION COSTS

The following cost breakdown is based on the initial purchase of a pre-war vintage Ford at an arbitrary price of $75. Such automobiles are available in the Southern California area for that figure—in good running shape—and it is assumed a similar car can be purchased in other sections of the country for that or less.

ITEM	S1-A Cost	S-4 Cost
Automobile	75.00	75.00
Victress Body	595.00	695.00
Frame Alteration	100.00	....
Drive Shaft Change	25.00	....
Lowering		10.00
Grille	20.00	25.00
Hardware	35.00	35.00
Upholstery	100.00	100.00
Miscellaneous	100.00	100.00
TOTAL	$1050.00	$1040.00

FIBERGLASS PROVES ITS STRENGTH

Shown here is a Victress S1-A body shell, with no interior bracing, supporting the weight of two full grown men. Fiberglass is stronger than mild steel and CANNOT be dented! Scraped fenders and parking lot bruises result simply in scraped paint. Most remarkable of all, damage is done, even in the severest accidents, only to the area of impact, and repairs are extremely simple.

THE VICTRESS S1-A SPORT CAR CHASSIS

Since many builders do not have the facilities for frame modification, the Victress Company has developed a sturdy, well designed frame assembly kit. This frame is of a Ford frame thoroughly reconditioned and rebuilt to our specifications.

The frame is first disassembled, sand-blasted and checked for flaws or cracks. Then the frame is shortened to 99". The "X" member is relocated to give better weight distribution, and the center section is lowered to give additional leg room. The front motor mount constitutes an additoinal cross member which gives added strength. All work is done in a frame jig to assure perfect alignment.

The Frame kit consists of the following parts:
1. Victress S1-A Frame, 2. Front and rear engine mounts (Ford or Mercury), 3. Sturdy 2" Steel Cowl Support Bar with integral pedal mounts and upper steering column support, 4. Master brake cylinder mount, 5. Lower steering mount, 6. Brake line brackets, 7. Special front radius rods and mounts, 8. Special shortened drive shaft and drive shaft housing, 9. Special rear radius rods.

No other custom parts of a major nature are needed to complete the Victress S1-A. All other parts used are standard over-the-counter items and can be purchased locally. Shipping weight, approx. 400 lbs.; price $295.00.

A Victress ready for competition

PRICE LIST AND SHIPPING DATA

Victress S1-A-1 (Basic Kit)
    Completely molded body including hood panel and one door. (Please specify right or left door.) ... $595.00
    Same body with two doors ... 625.00
    Rear Trunk Panel cut out with molded drip gutter ... 30.00

Victress S1-A-1F (Finished Kit)
    Same as S1-A-1 but includes hardware for door and hood, and body is trimmed, primed and ready to mount ... 695.00
    Above body with two doors, including hardware ... 745.00
    Rear deck with all hardware including lock and key ... 50.00

Victress S-4 (Basic Kit)
    Body completely molded with two doors, hood and rear deck panel fitted and all mounting brackets ... 695.00

Victress S-4F (Finished Kit)
    Same body as above but includes all door, hood and deck latches and body is trimmed and primed, ready to mount ... 795.00
    Finished kits of both models also include windshield frames.

Floor Sections
    For those who do not wish to take the time to construct their own floor section, we offer a pre-fab section for the S1-A which will fit Victress, Mameco and Kurtis frames. For the S-4, we offer a pre-fab section for '41-'48 Ford frames. These Pre-fab floor sections include cockpit floor, firewall and seat rest and are priced at $85.00. We will also construct floor sections to individual specifications, but in these cases, we must know (1) Distance from top of frame to ground with full load; (2) Distance from front of firewall to center of front axle, as all floor sections are mounted in the body before leaving our plant.

NOTE: Prices do not include federal and local taxes where applicable.

When ordering a Victress body, please specify frame you plan to use.

Shipping Data
    Crating Charge is $45.00. Shipping weight of S1-A is 550 lbs; the shipping weight of the S-4 is 650 lbs. Shipping charges, coast to coast are approximately $9.00 per hundred lbs. Proportionately less for shorter distances. All products are shipped via National Carloading where possible.

OTHER ITEMS AVAILABLE

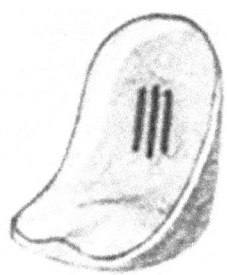 

Victress S-5 Body. Designed for 92" to 94" wheelbase. Similar in appearance to S1-A. Will fit MG's, Singers, Hillman-Minx, etc. Send for further information $545.00
Bucket Seats, fiberglass, racing type. Complete with metal mounting lugs 19.95
Anderson Crash Helmets. So safe they have the endorsement of Dr. Sydney Senter, AAA Track Physician. Small, medium, large, extra large 28.30
Victress S1-A Top. Fiberglass, Jag Bubble type 50.00
Experimental Fiberglass Kit. Sufficient materials to make 5 square feet of laminate, the kit includes a quart of resin, a yard each of matte and cloth and acetate film plus activating agents, and simplified instructions 6.95
Fiberglass Cloth, bulk. 38" wide, per yard 1.30
    44" Wide, per yard 1.45
    60" Wide, per yard 2.22
Fiberglass Matte, per square yard .... .75
Resin, per gallon 6.60
    5 gallons 21.34
Catalyst, enough for one gallon 1.40
    Enough for 5 gallons 4.00
Cobalt Napthanate, for one gallon .... .30
    Enough for 5 gallons 1.25

The Guy Mabee "Streetliner" ... 203 MPH Plus!

BODY BY Victress

MANUFACTURING COMPANY

11823 Sherman Way • North Hollywood, Calif.

1956 Brochure

1956 Tri-Fold Brochure (last 2 pages)

THE VICTRESS STORY

In a little over two years, the Victress Manufacturing Company has grown from a dream of William Boyce-Smith, its founder, to a business reality.

Today, the Victress Manufacturing Company is in production on more models than any other fiberglass body builder, and constantly seeking new models to please the public. It is this intense desire to continue advancement, not to be satisfied with just one body, that is responsible for the position of leadership which Victress enjoys.

The leadership of the Company is in the hands of three men who are well qualified for the position they hold. With backgrounds in plastics and the automotive field, it is quite natural that they have been able to present products to the market that are not only completely functional but also lastingly engineered.

William Boyce-Smith, known in West Coast Automotive circles as "Doc," was bitten by the auto bug in 1938, and built his first roadster that year. Its '29 A body was a far cry from the Victress bodies his firm builds today, but it performed well and Doc raced it, and other roadsters, at all Southern California Lakes meets, until the war put a stop to such activity. After the war, Doc raced in all CRA tracks and still found time to graduate from UCLA in engineering. His introduction to the magic world of fiberglass came in 1950, when he went to work for Lockheed's Plastic Division. After nearly three years of study and experimentation with the new material, Doc founded Victress Manufacturing Company. Today he is President and Chief Engineer of the firm.

Merrill Powell, Vice President and Design Group Chief for Victress, also spent a good portion of his life with roadsters and rods, but his interests turned more to design than racing. After graduating from Baylor, he took two years of Post Graduate work in Automotive Design at Los Angeles' famed Art Center School. Not yet 30, Powell is one of America's top up-and-coming designers, and is well known in automotive design circles.

Bill Powell—who is, incidentally, no relation to Merrill—is Production Manager and Competition Design Specialist for the firm. A familiar figure at California meets, Bill is considered one of the best lamination technicians in the business. The Dragster, a body designed strictly for sprint cars, is Bill's baby, and many hours of careful engineering were put in by him before the design was nailed down.

The employees of the firm are each specialists in some phase of fiberglass work; the sum total of all this know-how assures the purchaser of any Victress product that he will receive a body that is the ultimate in design, engineering and manufacturing skill.

The S-1A Victress' 99" wheelbase sports car body is unique in may ways ... it is one of few fiberglass sports car bodies ever wind tunnel tested for aerodynamic qualities and high speed stability ... it is the fastest sports car body in the world ... Its roominess is unparalled in the sports car field.

Over 4000 hours were put into the design and construction of the prototype S-1A. The result of this time, the production model S-1A, certainly justifies all the care that it was given.

In an effort to produce a body suitable for use on a standard wheelbase frame, with the barest minimum of chassis alterations, the S-2 and S-3 projects were launched. The problem was not a simple one (As evidenced by the fact that NO OTHER COMPANY HAS BEEN ABLE TO PRODUCE SUCH A BODY) for several reasons. To begin with, standard frame heights are such as to make low body silhouette a tough goal to reach. Furthermore, the very length of the standard

MERRILL, BILL AND DOC EXAMINE AN S-1A.

chassis would make some low designs look altogether too long ... yet the body had to be considerably lower than the standard body in order to achieve a modern appearance. The S-2 was carried to the mock-up stage and discarded because it looked too long. The S-3 was initiated on different design principles and refined, in its final stages, into the Victress S-4, a body primarily built to fit stock Ford frames, but also generally adaptable to other frames with a minimum of effort.

BILL POWELL'S DREAM—
THE VICTRESS DRAGSTER.

While many purists would disagree with the notion, it has long been the opinion of the Victress officials that a car which performs as well as the MG should be aerodynamically clean, too. Accordingly, the S-5 was designed and built. Bearing a strong family resemblance to its big sister, the S-1A, the S-5 not only improves the looks of an MG, it actually improves the performance as well, due to its streamlining and lower weight. A Victress-MG is not only a tough one to beat, it's a tough one to catch.

The Dragster began life as a personal project of Production Manager Bill Powell ... he needed a body for his own Drag machine. At first it was planned as a one-of-a-kind, but when drag enthusiasts began showing keen interest in the car, it was redesigned as a limited production model.

Several new Victress models are currently in planning stages, as the Victress Manufacturing Company constantly strives to maintain its leadership in the field. Victress is proud of its position, but will not forget the responsibility that leadership demands ... responsibility to you, the public.

THE VICTRESS S-1A

Beauty of line, functional design and thrilling performance mark it as America's most EVERYTHING sports car body!

The S-1A, America's fastest sports car body, was not the result of accidental discovery. The design—the first auto body ever built with an eye to combining sports car looks with streamliner aerodynamics— was the culmination of two years of research and engineering.

Wind tunnel tests gave laboratory evidence that the Victress S1-A was going to be the hottest thing on sports car wheels, but it remained for the Guy Mabee Special to prove this in the field.

At Bonneville, during the 1953 Nationals, Joe Mabee piloted the Special—with body by Victress—on a blistering two-way trip through the timing lights. The speed attained was a sizzling 203.105 MPH! Thus, without doubt, the Victress S-1A is America's fastest sports car body.

The streamlining and performance of this body, designed primarily for street operation, has given it the nickname of the "Streetliner."

Built by the sandwich laminate method (the strongest type of fiberglass construction), the S-1A is designed to fit a 99" wheelbase chassis. The chassis of any popular American car can be easily adapted to this wheelbase dimension, or an inexpensive ready-made chassis can be purchased from the Victress Company. In either case, the weight and lowering modifications give the resulting car added roadability and the handling characteristics of some of the finest European sports cars.

The modifications of standard frames can be accomplished by any blacksmith at a cost under $100. The necessary drive shaft modification can be done by any machine shop for $15 to $25. The body is mounted to the frame by easily installed angle brackets, and no phase of the work offers difficulties. Any person can, with a minimum of tools and know-how, do the work himself.

A wide variety of power plants have been used in cars constructed with Victress bodies, and any power plant is suitable.

Wheelbase 99"
Height above ground 38"
Width 67"
Seats 3

Engine Any desired
Frame Any Suitable
O/A Length 168"
Hood Opening 52"

(LEFT) HIGH ANGLE VIEW OF AN S-1A, AMERICA'S MOST BEAUTIFUL SPORTS CAR.
(RIGHT) MERRILL POWELL DRIVES HIS S-1A TO WORK.

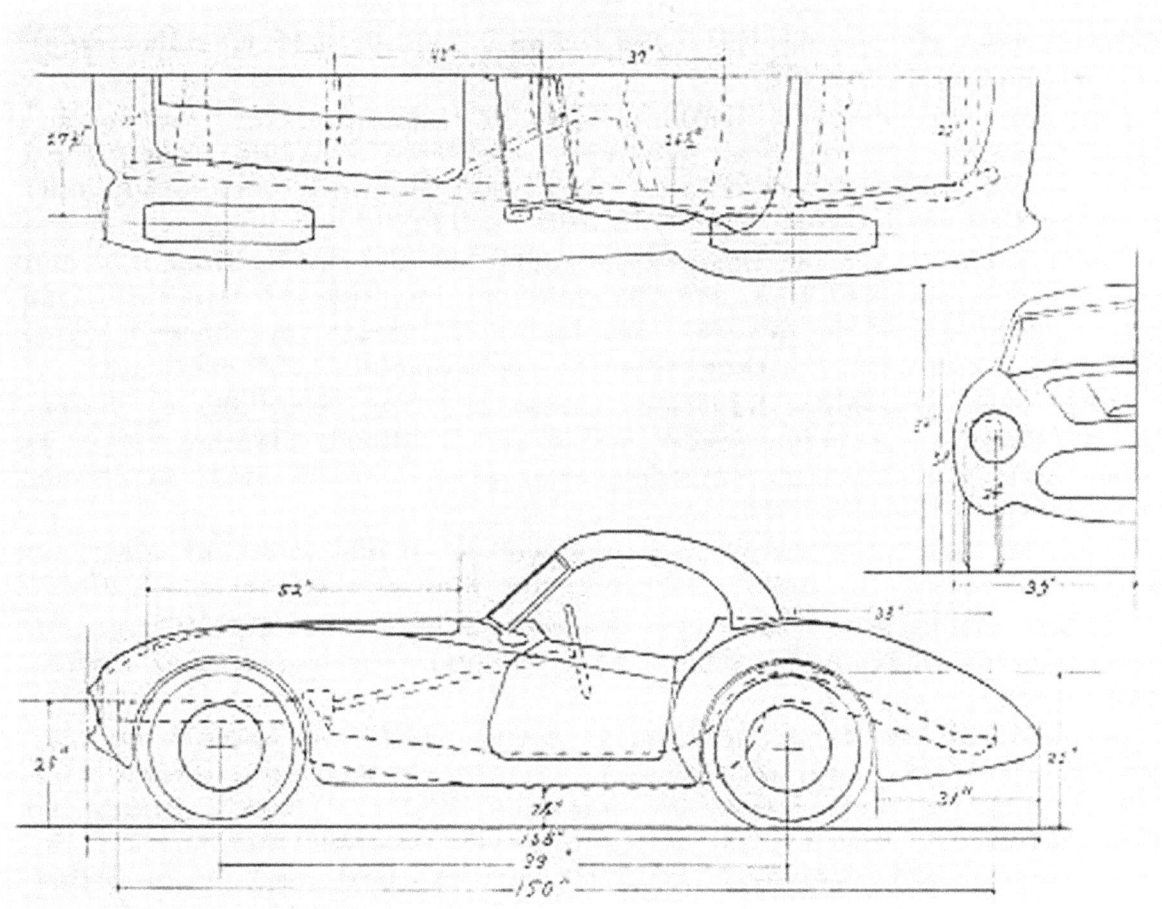

Engineering drawing of the Victress S-1A Body, showing important dimensions. The frame, shown by dotted lines in plan and side views, is a 1941 Ford frame modified to Victress specifications. You can have this work done on any frame, or you can purchase frames directly from Victress.

THE VICTRESS S-4

Converts stock car into the sports car category with the least amount of work ... and with stunning results.

The goal of building a fiberglass sport body to fit ANY of the popular priced American frames presented many problems. Wheelbases vary from 110" to 116"; suspension systems and motor mountings also vary considerably in the Fords, Chevrolets and Plymouths from 1940 to date.

These problems seemed almost insurmountable, but, by constant trial and error, fitting and re-fitting and dimensioning hundreds of tolerances, the basic proportions of the S-4 were developed. This phase saw the building of four scale models and the expenditure of approximately 1000 man hours.

After basic dimensions had been established, the actual job of designing a clean-lined, aerodynamically stable and artistically pleasing body was turned over to the Victress industrial design group. Two thousand man hours later, the design was finished.

The final result, the Victress S-4, was well worth the effort. Its crisp lines and low silhouette are greeted with admiring glances everywhere it is driven.

Its low weight/power ratio (the S-4 body is approximately 1000 pounds lighter then the stock body) gives it truly stunning performance using a purely stock engine.

An ingenious rear fender well design allows it to fit any frame in the 112" to 116" wheelbase range with minimum alteration to the stock member. In all, the only running gear alterations suggested by the Victress Company are those involved in lowering the frame-to-ground distance. The lowering process takes fullest advantage of the S-4's sweeping lines, and can be accomplished easily by any of the normal lowering methods such as use of lowering blocks, long shackles or reversing or torching springs.

Any auto shop can do this work for a very small amount, and the job of mounting the lightweight laminate body (weighs less than 200 pounds yet is as strong as steel!) is easily accomplished by anyone.

S - 4 SPECIFICATIONS

Wheelbase	112-116"	Engine	any desired
Height above ground	40½"	Frame	112"-116" W.B.
Width	70"	O/A Length	187"
Seats	3	Hood opening	55"

(LEFT) NOTE TAILLIGHT FAIRING AND GRACEFUL REAR FENDER SWEEP. (RIGHT) ANT'S-EYE VIEW OF INTERESTING S-4 GRILLE TREATMENT.

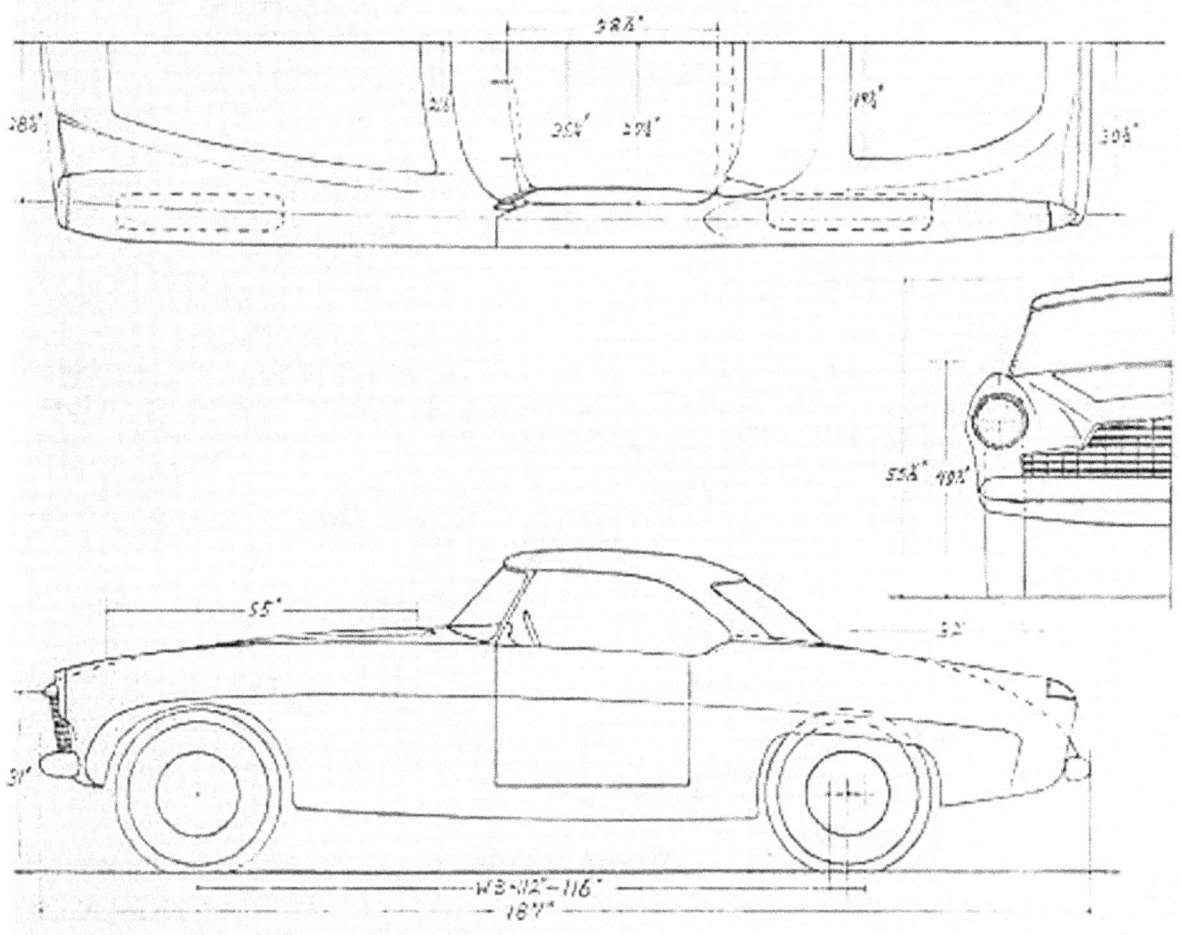

These drawings show some of the dimensions of the Victress S-4. Headlights represented here are 1953 Studebaker units, tail lights are 1952 Willys, and the suggested windshield is from a 1953 Ford convertible. Windshield frame is included with all

THE VICTRESS S-5

Filling a definite need in the motoring world, the S-5 makes the TC or TD or TF MG as pretty as a picture...notably improves performance, too!

The Victress Company, an ardent admirer of the superb performance and handling characteristics of the MG, has designed a body with beauty to match this performance.

The addition of a Victress S-5 body to an MG produces one of the finest acting and finest looking sport cars in the world, gives you a car with the looks of the expensive sports car class instead of the lower priced look.

Performance, too, is obviously increased. Not only does the highly streamlined S-5 body offer a great reduction in wind resistance and thereby appreciably increase top speed, its lower weight — (five-hundred pounds less than the stock member) brings the center of gravity closer to the ground for better four wheel stability, and, naturally, gives you more HP per pound of weight. This translates directly into more power at the wheels, gives you greater acceleration at all speeds.

All of which adds up to handling qualities superior to the already superb characteristics of the stock car.

The S-5 uses standard MG seats, or you may design your own interior. The body fits the stock MG chassis with no difficulty, requires a minimum of effort.

The engine compartment is roomy enough to accommodate most V-8 engines.

Frame kits and cut down axles—for those desiring to build a smaller sports car from scratch are available, too. See next page.

S - 5 SPECIFICATIONS

Wheelbase	94"		Engine	MG— most V-8s
Height above ground		34"	Frame	MG-94" W.B.
Width	60"		O/A Length	158"
Seats	2		Hood Opening	48"

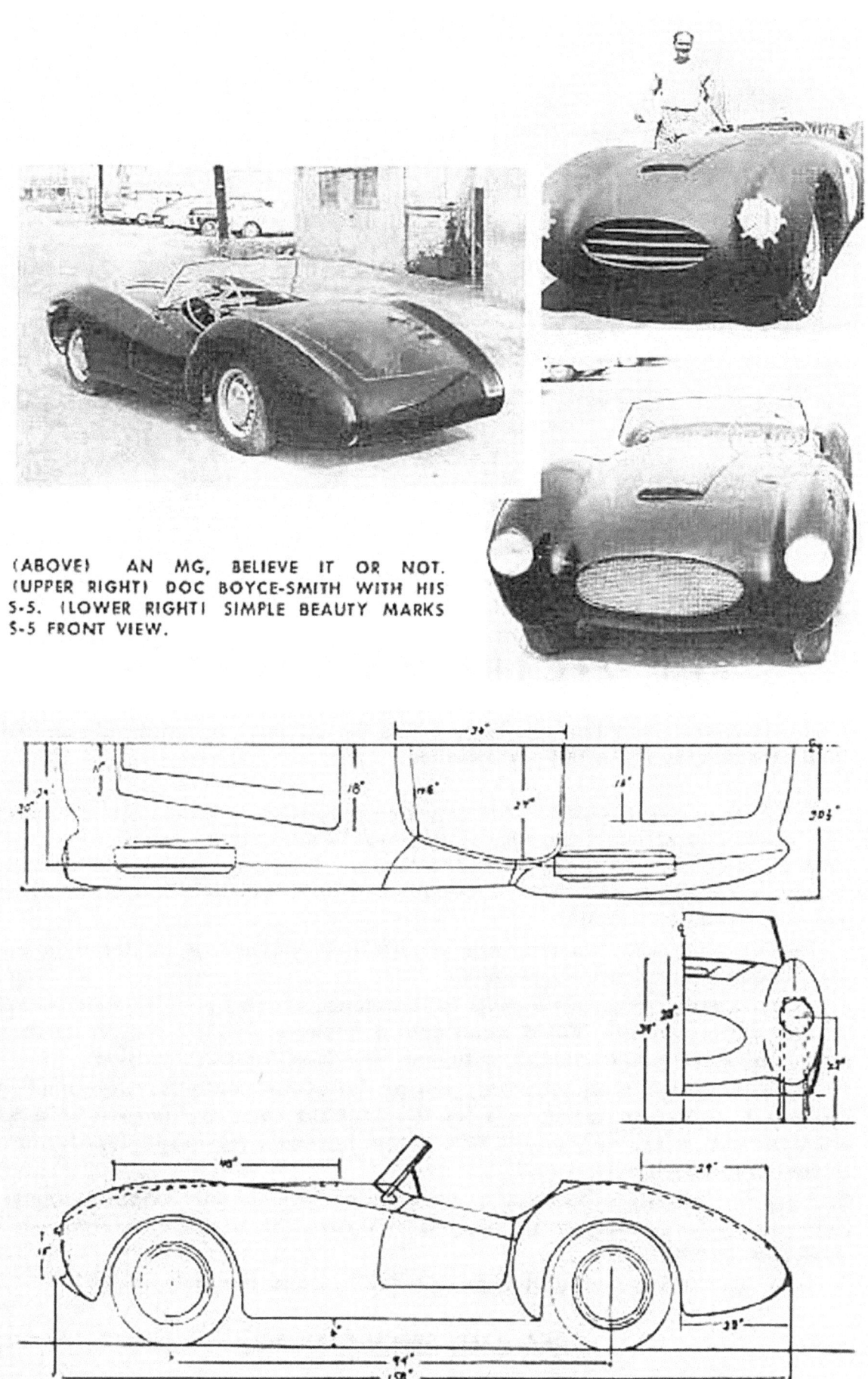

(ABOVE) AN MG, BELIEVE IT OR NOT. (UPPER RIGHT) DOC BOYCE-SMITH WITH HIS S-S. (LOWER RIGHT) SIMPLE BEAUTY MARKS S-S FRONT VIEW.

Diagram indicates body mounted on MG TD chassis, lowered 2" front and rear. Wheel wells will accept tires up to 6:70-15, as used on narrowed Ford axles.

THE VICTRESS DRAGSTER

Mean, low, nasty looking, this body offers the ultimate in lightweight streamlining essential to top sprint performance.

The Dragster was designed for only one purpose... short distance speed. The cockpit, practically on top of the rear wheels, puts your body weight where it does the most good in a sprint car... the long nose, sweeping down to only 14" high at the front, is designed to hold the front end down by air pressure instead of weight.

The Dragster body weighs approximately 40 pounds, is lighter than any other body construction would permit.

Its cowl design gives a minimum of turbulence at this point, deflects enough air around the cockpit that a windshield is unnecessary. The cockpit is roomy and sidewalls are low enough to permit driving with elbows outside.

The tail section is an anti-drag design based on contours established by Victress in designing racing tails for Indianapolis cars; its minimum drag coefficient falls in the 100 to 150 MPH range, however, making it ideal for drag racing and quarter mile events.

Thus, the Dragster offers you a sprint body which not only is good looking—and fast looking—but which also will improve the overall performance of your quarter-miler.

Take her through the traps once or twice... and see for yourself.

DRAGSTER SPECIFICATIONS

Wheelbase	100" — 118"	Engine	Any
Heigth above ground	Cowl 39"	Frame	any desired
Width	28"	O/A Length	174"

(ABOVE) A DRAGSTER ALL SET TO ROLL.
(RIGHT) A REAR VIEW SHOWING THE DRAGSTER'S EXCEPTIONALLY CLEAN LINES.

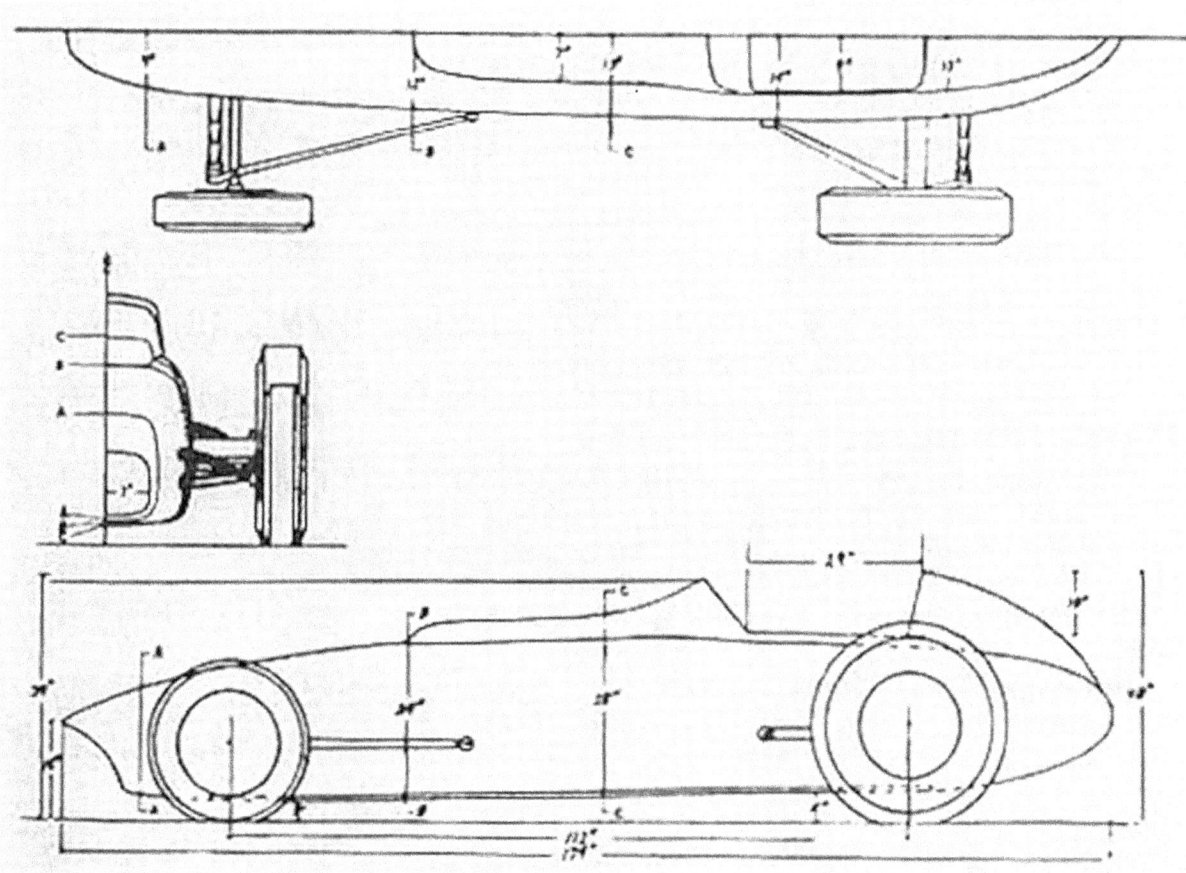

Body shell has no cut outs for running gear. Wheel base may vary from 100" to 118". Engine compartment is 24" minimum width—26" maximum. Height (with 3" ground clearance) is 28" inside body shell. Belly pan may be made of sheet aluminum, bowed to fit. Aluminum need not be hammered to shape.

VICTRESS-MAMECO FRAMES & FRAME KITS
Leader in Frames now produces chassis engineered to Victress bodies

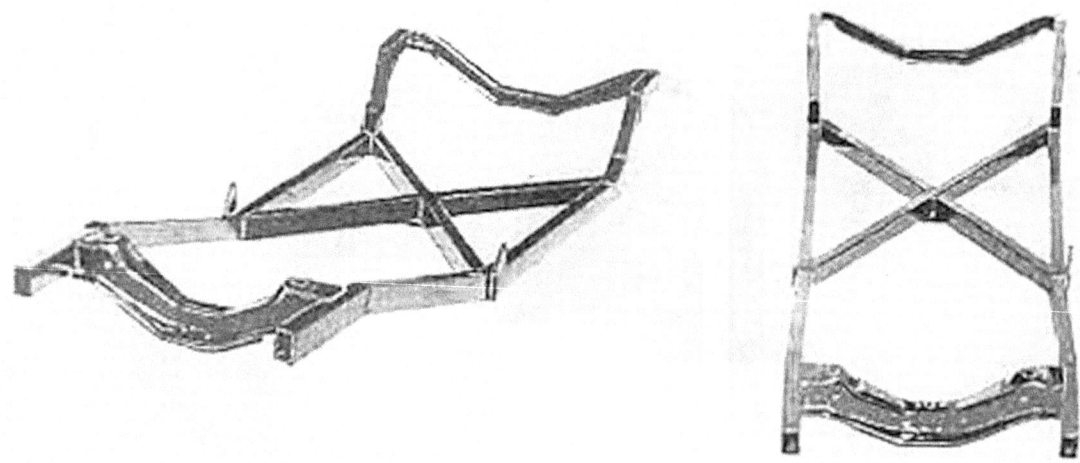

Victress Manufacturing Company can now offer those who want to build a sports car from scratch, as it were, a world-famous Mameco built frame, designed specifically for the Victress body.

In the engineering of these frames, the Mameco Company has bent every effort to create a chassis suitable for use in the highest performance sports car.

Mameco frames have been road tested under the most severe conditions imaginable; their strength has never wavered. They have been tested exhaustively in competition, and their superb balance and remarkable handling characteristics class them with the best European chassis.

Victress-Mameco frames may be purchased alone, or in complete kits.

The bare frame has been designed to use standard, easily obtainable, '39-'48 Ford parts. The assembly of all running gear onto the frame offers no difficulties, as easy-to-follow instructions are included with every frame.

The frame kit comes complete with all the necessary parts included. All special work—such as shortening torque tube and drive shaft, modifying steering column and radius arms, etc—has been done. The only work entailed with a frame kit is simple bolt-on assembly work.

Frames and frame kits are available in either 99" W.B. or 94" W.B. to fit the Victress S-1A body or the Victress S-5 body.

The frame has the following parts integral with it: (1) Pedal assembly; (2) Front and rear motor mounts; (3) Front and rear shock absorber mounts; (4) Front radius arm mounts; (5) Body mounts; (6) Master cylinder mount; (7) Steering gear mount; (8) Battery Box; (9) Thrust reactor rod mounts; (10) Radiator mounts; (11) Brake line mounting brackets; (12) Bottoming pads.

The frame kit in addition contains: (1) Torque tube shortened, with mounts for radius arms, brake lines, emergency brake, and drive shaft, shortened and re-splined; (2) Rear radius arms shortened and modified with emergensy brake bell cranks installed; (3) Front radius arms split and modified; (4) New lengthened Ford steering worm and shaft; (5) Special steering mast jacket; (6) Special long Pitman arm for faster steering ratio; (7) Drag link sleeve lengthened; (8) Special rear main spring leaf; (9) Two special thrust reactor rods; (10) Special clutch and brake activating rods; (11) Instructions for assembly.

FLOOR SECTIONS

For those who do not wish to construct their own cockpit floor sections, Victress can do the work for them. These floor sections are built of sturdy 3/4 inch plywood, are precision cut and fitted and laminated right into the Victress body of your choice before shipment. The floor section for the S-1 will fit the Victress-Mameco frame; the floor section for the S-4 is designed to fit '41-48 Ford frames; the section for the S-5 fits MG frames or the Victress-Mameco 94" WB chassis.

The floor sections include firewall, cockpit floor and seat rest, and are priced at $75.00. Custom sections, designed to individual specifications will be built by Victress on special quote, but, in these cases, customer must furnish drawings and dimensions, including (a) distance from top of frame to ground with full load and (b) distance from front of firewall to center of front axle.

SHIPPING & CRATING DATA

Crating charges on Victress bodies is $45.00; crating charges on Victress-Mameco frames is $10.00. There is no frame crating charge when frames are purchased with bodies. Shipping weight of S1-A is 550 lbs; the shipping weight of the S-4 is 650 lbs. Shipping charges, coast to coast are approximately $9.00 per hundred lbs. Proportionately less for shorter distances. All products are shipped via National Carloading where possible.

FIBERGLASS PROVES ITS STRENGTH

Shown here is a Victress S1-A body shell, with no interior bracing, supporting the weight of two full grown men. Fiberglass is stronger than mild steel and CANNOT be dented! Scraped fenders and parking lot bruises result simply in scraped paint. Most remarkable of all, damage is done, even in the severest accidents, only to the area of impact, and repairs are extremely simple.

VICTRESS PICTURE PAGE

1. THE GUY MABEE SPECIAL, AT 203 PLUS MPH—WORLD'S FASTEST SPORTS CAR. 2. THE DESIGNED VICTRESS INTERIOR. 3. S-1A AND DC-3. 4. AN S-5 READY FOR COMPETITION 5. THE DRAGSTER AT DESERT MEET. 6. THE VICTRESS S-4.—BEAUTY AT ANY ANGLE

66

PRICE LIST

BODIES & FRAMES

S-1A—Completely molded with one door, (either side) and hood.	$ 595.00
Additional Door	30.00
Rear Deck Lid	30.00
S-1AF—As above but with windshield frames and hardware installed, primed and ready to paint	695.00
Additional Door with Hardware installed	50.00
Rear Deck Lid, Hardware installed	50.00
S-1AFK—Same as S-1AF but includes frame and floor section	945.00
S-1AKF2—Same as S-1AF but includes complete Victress-Mameco Frame Kit and floor section	1173.00
S-4—Completely molded with two doors, hood and rear Deck Lid	695.00
S-4F—As above, but with windshield frames and hardware installed; primed and ready to paint	795.00
S-5—Completely molded with one door, (either side) and hood	575.00
Additional door	30.00
Rear Deck Lid	30.00
S-5F—As above but with windshield frames and hardware installed, primed and ready to paint	675.00
Additional Door with Hardware Installed	50.00
Rear Deck Lid, Hardware Installed	50.00
DRAGSTER—Completely molded and trimmed, with plastic supplies for mounting brackets & firewall	250.00

NOTE: A generous supply of plastic materials—enough for limited customizing, repairs, or firewall and floorboard installation—is included with all body kits.

VICTRESS MAMECO FRAMES—99" Frame	208.38
99" Frame Kit, as described in Frame Section	483.33
94" Frame, with 50" tread to use Ford Components with Victress S-5 Body	208.38
94" Frame Kit, described in Frame section	560.08

NOTE: All Frames and Frame Kits are sold outright, no exchange parts being required.

BUCKET SEATS, including mounting brackets, fiberglass	19.50
FLOOR SECTIONS	75.00

HARDWARE LIST

Windshield Frames, S-1A, S-4, or S-5	25.00
Hood Hinge Assembly	7.50
Deck Hinge Assembly	7.50
Door Hinge Assembly	7.75
Deck Lock or Hood Lock	2.50
Door Latch Assembly	4.00

FIBERGLASS MATERIALS

Fiberglass Cloth, 38" wide, per yard	1.10
Fiberglass Matte, 38", 1½ oz. weight, per yard	1.10
Resin, five gallon size only	27.50
Catalyst, enough for 5 gallons of Resin	4.50
Cobalt, enough for 5 gallons of Resin	1.75
Parting Agent, gallon size only	5.50

NOTE: As we are a manufacturer, not a supplier, and sell these materials only as a courtesy, we must limit sales of Fiberglass Materials to orders of $75.00 minimum and over

Victress
Sport Car Bodies

Frame Kit FOR S-1A ROADSTER AND C-3 COUPE.

For those who do not wish to invest the time and effort necessary to modify a stock frame we now offer a complete frame kit. This kit is designed to be used with 1939 – 1948 Ford running gear and chassis parts. Frame kit includes:
1. A rugged frame constructed from 2" x 3" square tubing to insure maximum rigidity; 2. Shortened torque tube and drive shaft; 3. Rear radius rods with emergency bell-crank installed; 4. Two special front radius arms; 5. New Ford steering worm and shaft reworked to fit frame; 6. Steering mast jacket; 7. Special pitman arm for faster steering ratio; 8. Special drag link; 9. New low arch rear main spring leaf; 10. Two thrust reactor rods; 11. Clutch and brake activating rods; 12. Instructions for assembly.

Complete Kit: $ 475.00 plus excise tax.
Frame Only: $ 195.50 plus excise tax.

Adaptable Stock Components

Many variations in trim, grille and accessories can be used with Victress bodies. The individual tastes of each builder will dictate the final choice. Various combinations of standard trim and accessories can be used to make the finished Victress truly a custom car. Listed below are some of the more commonly used units.

S-1A – WINDSHIELD – "V" type flat glass fits frames provided. Corvette or Thunderbird (frame and glass), 1950 Olds 88 (trimmed 4" in width).
HEADLIGHTS – Standard 1941 to 1948 Ford.
GRILLE – 1952 Packard (narrowed 6"), 1953 Chev. center bar, 1955 Chev. grille, "Egg Crate" aluminum strips, parallel chrome tubes.

S-5 – Basically similar to S-1A.

C-3 – WINDSHIELD – 1954 Plymouth convertible.
HEADLIGHTS – 1952 Buick or Olds.
SIDE WINDOWS – Glass must be cut to fit. Window lifts mechanism is completely assembled from rear side window of 1949 Ford Tudor.
REAR WINDOW – Molded by Victress from Plexiglas.

S-4 – WINDSHIELD – Standard 1952 Ford.
HEADLIGHTS – 1952 Studebaker or same rims can be adapted to 1941 – 1948 Ford unit.
GRILLE – No stock grille will fit. Use "Egg Crate" style, parallel bars, etc.

Ordering and Shipping

All Victress bodies are built to order. A deposit of $200.00 is required with your order and the balance is due at time of shipment. Body will be shipped approximately 21 days from receipt of order.

Crating charge – $45.00.

All orders are subject to 10% Federal Excise Tax.

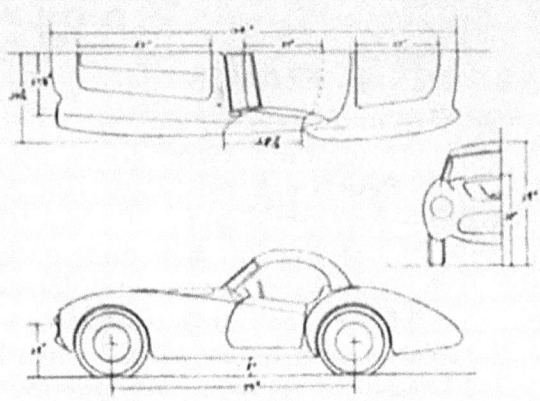

Victress S-1A Roadster

Caution ....

Do not attempt to complete the chassis and running gear before you have the body on hand. It is always best to check the progress of the work by repeated fitting of the body as the job proceeds. Quarter inch and half inch errors make a great deal of re-working necessary when your Victress body arrives. Planning and general lay-out can be completed and all major components can be jigged in place with clamps, etc., but no final welding should be attempted.

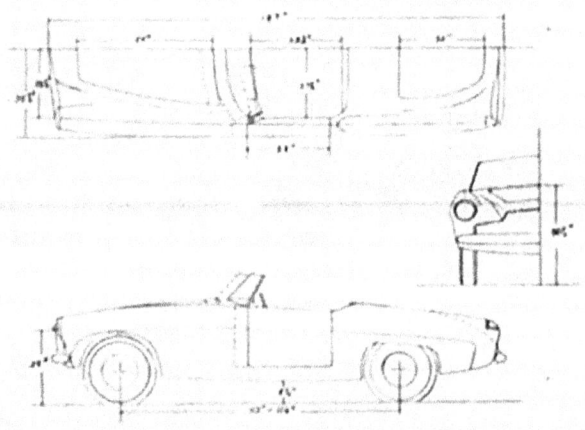

Victress S-4 Roadster

Dotted line indicates windshield and door position on five passenger type.

Victress C-3 Coupe

Victress Manufacturing Company, Inc., 11823 Sherman Way, North Hollywood, California

1957
Hellings Flyer

Hellings Company

AUTHORIZED OUTLET FOR THE *VICTRESS Sport Car BODY*

HERE'S HOW!

This is all you have to do to modify standard auto frames to fit the new VICTRESS Fiberglas SPORT CAR BODY:

Stock Ford frame

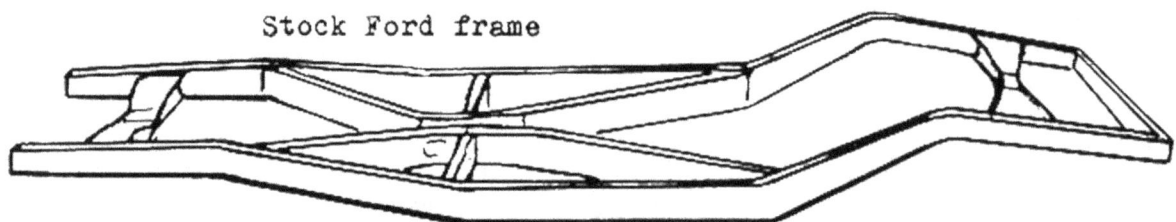

1. Remove entire "X" section

2. Cut frame in four places as shown:

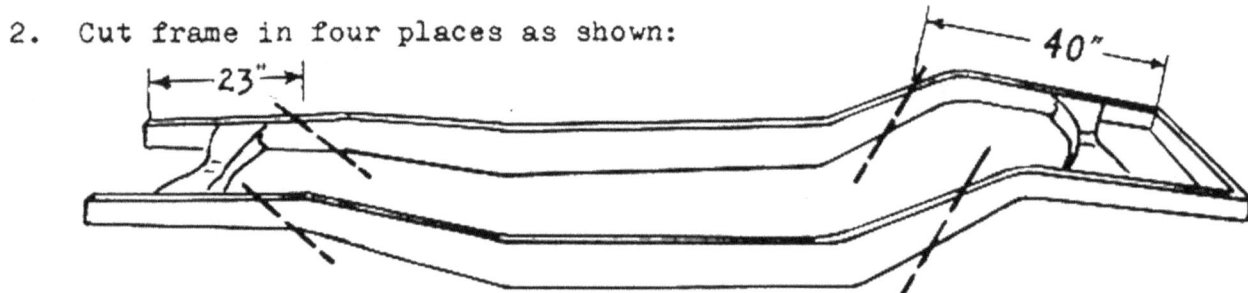

3. Overlap frame so that wheelbase is 100 inches, then weld. Add reinforcing plates (shown by dotted lines).

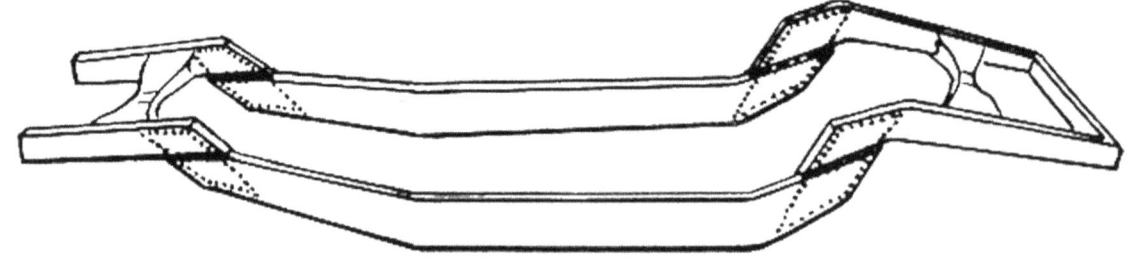

4. Re-locate "X" section

   Do this by mounting frame on front and rear end assemblies; positioning engine, transmission, and shortened drive-shaft; then fit "X" section. Weld in place.

HELLINGS CO.

11423 VANOWEN STREET
NORTH HOLLYWOOD, CALIFORNIA

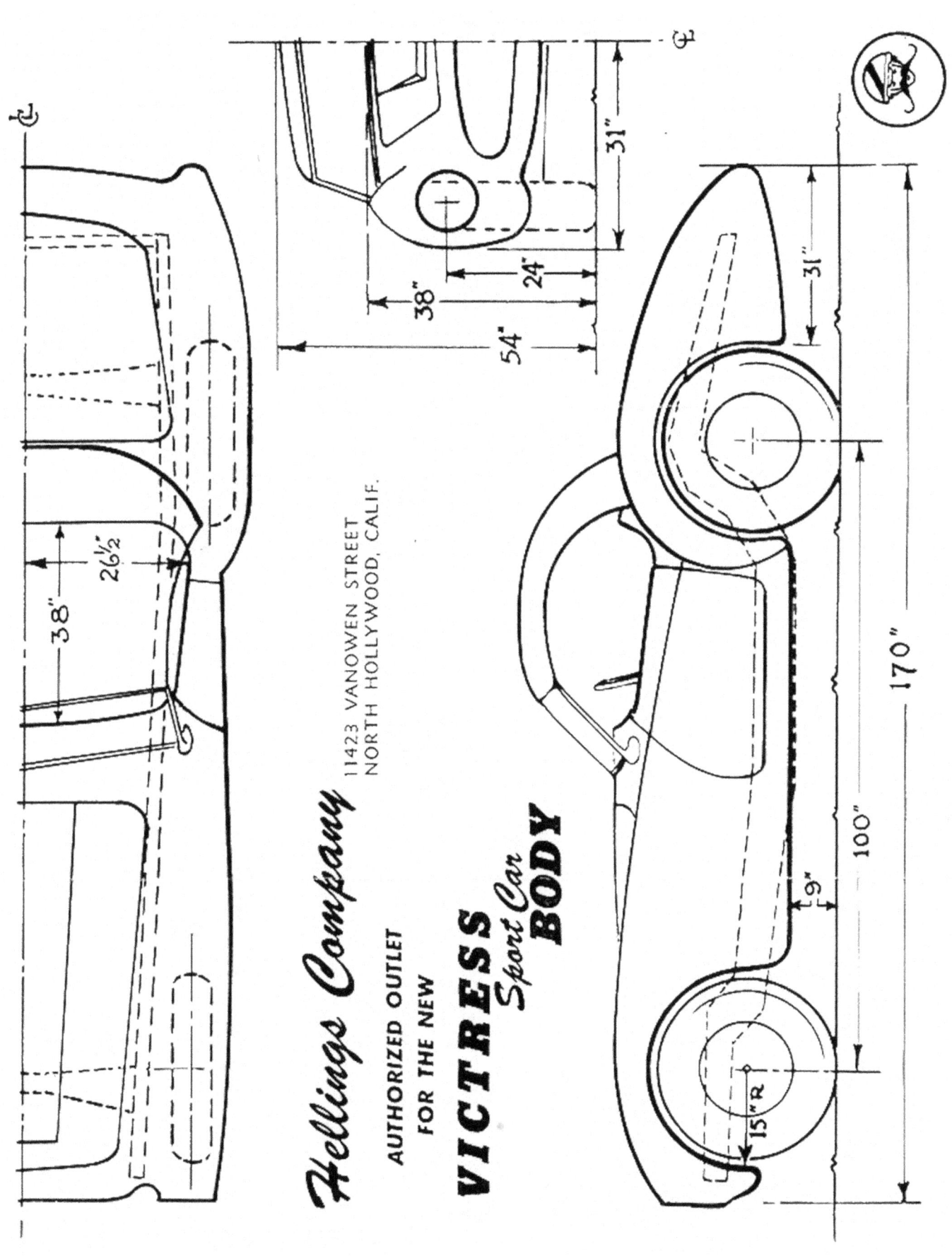

1960
Brochure
(Single Sheet Double Sided)

Victress Sport Car Bodies

Basic Body.....
- Completely formed fiberglass shell, trimmed on all edges.

Standard Kit.....
- Completely formed fiberglass body, trimmed on all edges.
- Molded drain gutters on hood and deck.
- Sturdy box section reinforcement on hood, deck and doors.
- Hinges and latches installed and working on hood, deck and doors.
- Windshield posts (cast aluminum)
- TEMPLATE KIT:
    - Front and rear wheel wells
    - Firewall (two parts)
    - Floor boards
    - Back rest
    - Window lift mounts (coupe only)
- Resin and fiberglass supplies enough to make forty sq. ft. of fiberglass laminate.

ORDERING AND SHIPPING

All Victress and Byers bodies are built to order. A down payment of $200.00 is required with your order and the balance is due at time of shipment. Body will be shipped approximately 21 days from receipt of order.

Crating charge - $45.00

All bodies are subject to 10% Federal Excise Tax.

YOU CAN BUILD YOUR OWN **SPORT** *Car* FOR AS LITTLE AS **$1000.00**

ITEM 1	– VICTRESS S-4 BODY	$349.50*
ITEM 2	– 1939 THRU 1948 FORD CHASSIS	150.00
ITEM 3	– REPAIR WORN CHASSIS AND ENGINE PARTS	165.00
ITEM 4	– ALLOWANCE FOR MISC. PARTS AND FITTINGS	75.00
ITEM 5	– ALLOWANCE FOR PAINT JOB	60.00
ITEM 6	– ALLOWANCE FOR UPHOLSTERY	126.00
ITEM 7	– WINDSHIELD GLASS STD. 1953-1954 FORD SEDAN	35.00
ITEM 8	– GENERAL FIBERGLASS SUPPLIES	35.00
	TOTAL	$994.50

* Plus Tax

Now you can buy a VICTRESS fiberglass car body for as little as $295.00 plus tax. Only VICTRESS offers all these advantages: Blemish free surfaces; Easy to follow, step-by-step instructions with plenty of pictures; Generous fiberglass and plastic supplies with each kit; Rain gutters on hood and trunk lids. VICTRESS body kits are not just shells! Hood, trunk lid and doors are completely fabricated.

VICTRESS C-3 MODEL

W.B. 98" to 102" – Tread 58"
FOR MODIFIED FORD CHASSIS ..

BASIC BODY	$395.00
STD. KIT	$645.00

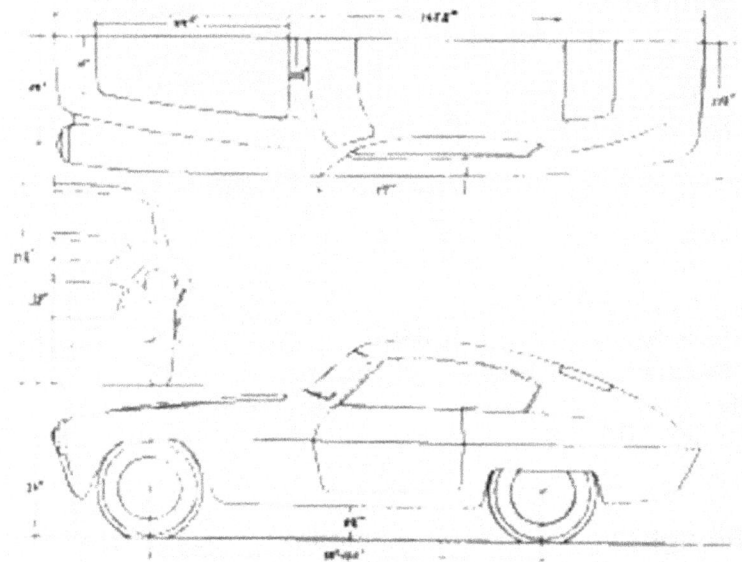

CAUTION ....

Do not attempt to complete the chassis and running gear before you have the body on hand. It is always best to check the progress of the work by repeated fittings of the body as the job proceeds. Quarter inch and half inch errors make a great deal of re-working necessary when your Victress body arrives. Planning and general lay-out can be completed and all major components can be jigged in place with clamps, etc., but no final welding should be attempted.

A SAMPLE LIST OF OTHER BOOKS AVAILABLE FROM

www.VelocePress.com

PLEASE CHECK OUR WEBSITE FOR THE MOST UP-TO-DATE INFORMATION

AUTOBOOKS SERIES OF WORKSHOP MANUALS

ALFA ROMEO GIULIA 1750, 2000 1962-1978 WORKSHOP MANUAL
AUSTIN HEALEY SPRITE, MG MIDGET 1958-1980 WORKSHOP MANUAL
BMW 1600 1966-1973 WORKSHOP MANUAL
FIAT 1100, 1100D, 1100R & 1200 1957-1969 WORKSHOP MANUAL
FIAT 124 1966-1974 WORKSHOP MANUAL
FIAT 124 SPORT 1966-1975 WORKSHOP MANUAL
FIAT 125 & 125 SPECIAL 1967-1973 WORKSHOP MANUAL
FIAT 126, 126L, 126DV, 126/650 & 126/650DV 1972-1982 WORKSHOP MANUAL
FIAT 127 SALOON, SPECIAL & SPORT, 900, 1050 1971-1981 WORKSHOP MANUAL
FIAT 128 1969-1982 WORKSHOP MANUAL
FIAT 1300, 1500 1961-1967 WORKSHOP MANUAL
FIAT 131 MIRAFIORI 1975-1982 WORKSHOP MANUAL
FIAT 132 1972-1982 WORKSHOP MANUAL
FIAT 500 1957-1973 WORKSHOP MANUAL
FIAT 600, 600D & MULTIPLA 1955-1969 WORKSHOP MANUAL
FIAT 850 1964-1972 WORKSHOP MANUAL
JAGUAR E-TYPE 1961-1972 WORKSHOP MANUAL
JAGUAR MK 1, 2 1955-1969 WORKSHOP MANUAL
JAGUAR S TYPE, 420 1963-1968 WORKSHOP MANUAL
JAGUAR XK 120, 140, 150 MK 7, 8, 9 1948-1961 WORKSHOP MANUAL
LAND ROVER 1, 2 1948-1961 WORKSHOP MANUAL
MERCEDES-BENZ 190 1959-1968 WORKSHOP MANUAL
MERCDEDS-BENZ 220/8 1968-1972 WORKSHOP MANUAL
MERCEDES-BENZ 230 1963-1968 WORKSHOP MANUAL
MERCEDES-BENZ 250 1968-1972 WORKSHOP MANUAL
MG MIDGET TA-TF 1936-1955 WORKSHOP MANUAL
MINI 1959-1980 WORKSHOP MANUAL
MORRIS MINOR 1952-1971 WORKSHOP MANUAL
PEUGEOT 404 1960-1975 WORKSHOP MANUAL
PORSCHE 911 1964-1969 WORKSHOP MANUAL
PORSCHE 911 1970-1977 WORKSHOP MANUAL
RENAULT 8, 10, 1100 1962-1971 WORKSHOP MANUAL
RENAULT 16 1965-1979 WORKSHOP MANUAL
ROVER 3500, 3500S 1968-1976 WORKSHOP MANUAL
SUNBEAM RAPIER, ALPINE 1955-1965 WORKSHOP MANUAL
TRIUMPH SPITFIRE, GT6, VITESSE 1962-1968 WORKSHOP MANUAL
TRIUMPH TR2, TR3, TR3A 1952-1962 WORKSHOP MANUAL
TRIUMPH TR4, TR4A 1961-1967 WORKSHOP MANUAL
VOLKSWAGEN BEETLE 1968-1977 WORKSHOP MANUAL

All VelocePress titles are available through your local independent bookseller, Amazon.com, or they may be purchased directly through our website at www.VelocePress.com. Wholesale customers may also purchase directly from us or from the Ingram Book Group.

MOTORCYCLE WORKSHOP MANUALS, MAINTENANCE & TECHNICAL TITLES

ARIEL WORKSHOP MANUAL 1933-1951
BMW FACTORY WORKSHOP MANUAL R26 R27 (1956-1967)
BMW FACTORY WSM R50 R50S R60 R69S R50US R60US R69US (1955-1969)
BSA SERVICE & REPAIR ALL PRE-WAR MODELS TO 1939, SV & OHV 150cc TO 1,000cc
DUCATI FACTORY WORKSHOP MANUAL SINGLE CYLINDER NARROW CASE OHC ENGINES 160cc, 250cc, 350cc - MONZA JUNIOR, MONZA, 250GT, MARK 3, MACH 1, MOTOCROSS & SEBRING
HONDA FACTORY WORKSHOP MANUAL 250cc TO 305cc C/CS/CB 72 & 77 SERIES 1960-1969
HONDA FACTORY WORKSHOP MANUAL 125cc TO 150cc C/CS/CB/CA 92 & 95 SERIES 1959-1966
HONDA FACTORY WORKSHOP MANUAL 50cc C110 SPORT CUB (1962-1969)
HONDA FACTORY WORKSHOP MANUAL 50cc C100 SUPER CUB
HONDA SERVICE & REPAIR 50cc TO 305cc C100, C102, MONKEY BIKE, CE 105H TRIALS BIKE, C110, C114, C92, CB92, BENLEY, C72, CB72, C77 & CB77
NORTON FACTORY WORKSHOP MANUAL 1957-1970
NORTON WORKSHOP MANUAL 1932-1939
ROYAL ENFIELD 736cc INTERCEPTOR & ENFIELD INDIAN CHIEF
SUZUKI T10 FACTORY WORKSHOP MANUAL 250cc 1963-1967
SUZUKI T20 & T200 FACTORY WORKSHOP MANUAL 200cc X-5 INVADER & STING RAY SCRAMBLER, 250cc X-6 HUSTLER 1965-1969
TRIUMPH FACTORY WORKSHOP MANUAL NO. 11 (1945-1955)
TRIUMPH WORKSHOP MANUAL 1935-1939
TRIUMPH WORKSHOP MANUAL 1937-1951
VESPA SERVICE & REPAIR ALL MODELS 125cc & 150cc 1951-1961
VINCENT SERVICE & REPAIR 1935-1955

CLASSIC AUTO TITLES & REFERENCE BOOKS

ABARTH BUYERS GUIDE
CARRERA PANAMERICANA 1950 ~ THE STORY OF THE 1950 MEXICAN ROAD RACE
DIALED IN ~ THE JAN OPPERMAN STORY
FERRARI 308 SERIES BUYER'S AND OWNER'S GUIDE
FERRARI BERLINETTA LUSSO
FERRARI BROCHURES & SALES LITERATURE 1946-1967
FERRARI SERIAL NUMBERS PART I ~ STREET CARS TO SERIAL # 21399 (1948-1977)
FERRARI SERIAL NUMBERS PART II ~ RACE CARS TO SERIAL # 1050 (1948-1973)
FERRARI SPYDER CALIFORNIA
IF HEMINGWAY HAD WRITTEN A RACING NOVEL ~ THE BEST OF MOTOR RACING FICTION 1950-2000
LE MANS 24 ~ WHAT THE MOVIE COULD HAVE BEEN
MASERATI BROCHURES AND SALES LITERATURE ~ POSTWAR THROUGH INLINE 6 CYLINDER CARS

All VelocePress titles are available through your local independent bookseller, Amazon.com, or they may be purchased directly through our website at www.VelocePress.com. Wholesale customers may also purchase directly from us or from the Ingram Book Group.

OTHER WORKSHOP MANUALS, MAINTENANCE & TECHNICAL TITLES

AUSTIN HEALEY SIX CYLINDER CARS 1956-1968
BMW ISETTA FACTORY REPAIR MANUAL
FERRARI 250/GT SERVICE AND MAINTENANCE
FERRARI GUIDE TO PERFORMANCE
FERRARI OPERATING, MAINTENANCE & SERVICE HANDBOOKS 1948-1963
FERRARI OWNER'S HANDBOOK
FERRARI TUNING TIPS & MAINTENANCE TECHNIQUES
METROPOLITAN WORKSHOP MANUAL
MASERATI OWNER'S HANDBOOK
OBERT'S FIAT GUIDE
PERFORMANCE TUNING THE SUNBEAM TIGER
PORSCHE 356 SERVICE AND MAINTENANCE MANUAL 1948-1965
PORSCHE 912 WORKSHOP MANUAL
SOUPING THE VOLKSWAGEN IMPROVING THE PERFORMANCE OF YOUR VW
TRIUMPH TR2, TR3 & TR4 WORKSHOP MANUAL
VOLVO ALL MODELS 1944-1968 WORKSHOP MANUAL

BROOKLANDS ROAD TEST PORTFOLIOS

FIAT DINO 1968-1973
MV AGUSTA F4 750 & 1000 1997-2007
JAGUAR MK1 & MK2 1955-1969
LOTUS CORTINA 1963-1970
FIAT 500 1936-1972
FERRARI ROAD CARS 1946-1956

All VelocePress titles are available through your local independent bookseller, Amazon.com, or they may be purchased directly through our website at www.VelocePress.com. Wholesale customers may also purchase directly from us or from the Ingram Book Group.

www.ingramcontent.com/pod-product-compliance
Lightning Source LLC
Chambersburg PA
CBHW080925170426
43201CB00016B/2263